THE
GUT REACTION
EATING PLAN

THE
GUT REACTION
EATING PLAN

*Choose, prepare and combine foods
to cleanse your system and revitalise
your health*

Gudrun Jonsson
with Tessa Rose

Vermilion
LONDON

First published in Great Britain in 2000

5 7 9 10 8 6 4

Text © Gudrun Jonsson 2000

First published by Vermilion, an imprint of Ebury Press
Random House, 20 Vauxhall Bridge Road, London SW1V 2SA

Random House Australia (Pty) Limited
20 Alfred Street, Milsons Point, Sydney,
New South Wales 2061, Australia

Random House New Zealand Limited
18 Poland Road, Glenfield,
Auckland 10, New Zealand

Random House (Pty) Limited
Endulini, 5a Jubilee Road, Parktown 2193, South Africa

The Random House Group Limited Reg. No. 954009

ISBN 0 09181981 4

A CIP catalogue record for this book
is available from the British Library

Papers used by Vermilion are natural, recyclable products
made from wood grown in sustainable forests.

Printed and bound in Great Britain by
Bookmarque Ltd, Croydon, Surrey

Although every effort has been made to ensure that the contents of
this book are accurate, it must not be treated as a susbstitute for
qualified medical advice. Always consult a qualified medical
practitioner. Neither the Author nor the Publisher can be held
responsible for any loss or claim arising out of the use, or misuse, of
the suggestions made or the failure to take medical advice.

It is in the shelter of each other that the people live
Irish Proverb

In loving memory of Nuala

ACKNOWLEDGEMENTS

My thanks to Fiona MacIntyre and Joanna Carreras at Ebury, to my perfect writing partner Tessa Rose and to Cath, to all at the Arcturus Agency, especially Ian McLellan, Louise Page and Jane Birch for all their support, inspiration and humour.

Thank you to Kathryn Hawkins, a wise cook, for all her help with the recipes. To Dr Schellander of the Liongate Clinic in Tunbridge Wells; Roger Wilson of Biopathica and Lennart Sedegard in Sweden.

CONTENTS

Introduction   ix

Chapter One: **The Fundamentals of Healthy Eating**   1
No Mean Machine   1
Understanding the Mechanics   3
The Liver   6
The Cinderella Problem   7
Absorbing the Basics   8

Chapter Two: **Into the Looking Glass**   9
With Friends Like These . . .   11
The Nanny State   12
The Blame Culture   14
The Bottom Line   15

Chapter Three: **What's Eating You?**   17
Indigestion   17
Wind   18
The Bermuda Triangle: Constipation, Diarrhoea and Irritated Bowel   19
Low Blood Sugar   21

Chapter Four: **The Eating Plans**   24
Repairing the Damage   24
Changing the Culture   27
Food for Thought   29
Constipation Eating Plan   32
Diarrhoea Eating Plan   37
Irritated Bowel Eating Plan   41

Chapter Five: **Recipes for the Eating Plans**   48
Basics   48
Main Meals: Constipation   51
Main Meals: Diarrhoea   56
Main Meals: IBS   59

Chapter Six: **Feeding Ideas**   64
Gudrun's Store Cupboard   65
Maintenance Recipes   72
Soups   72
Sauces and Dressings   76
Main Dishes   81
Puddings   89
Feeding the Future   94
Food Tips   99

Chapter Seven: **A–Zs of Opportunity**   102
Foods   102
Herbs   131
Supplements   137

Epilogue: **The Frailty Package**   143
Picking Yourself Up   143

Resources   145

Index   147

INTRODUCTION

When a sequel to my first book, *Gut Reaction*, was mooted it seemed logical for me to consider providing a blueprint for the ongoing management of various types of common weakness or susceptibility associated with the digestion. One of the most common questions I am asked at the end of a treatment programme is, 'Where do I go from here?' Taking supplements and having a strict regime to follow is easy in comparison with LAG (life after Gudrun), or so I am told. Decisions have to be taken about what food to eat, warning signals have to be looked for and acted upon, one has to begin taking responsibility for one's own digestion and divining its requirements. This is real life.

When looking at a health problem from the perspective of digestion there is always the danger that you might begin by throwing the baby out with the bath water. Food is not the demon of this piece and the road ahead is not impossibly narrow in dietary terms. There is nothing more irritating, I find, than the 'one size fits all' philosophy, and for this reason I was against the idea of this being merely a recipe book, a compilation of 'prescriptions' for healthy eating. Far from being useful, such books tend to demoralise people who like food by telling them what they should not eat and chastising them into acquiring a tolerance of the bland and uninteresting.

What you should eat depends on what state your body is in. Unfortunately, most people's guts are in a pretty poor shape. Half of the book is necessarily given over to explaining why this should be so, because unless we recognise our real selves fundamental change through diet is impossible. This book is about making food work for us. In order to do this we have to understand its effects and learn how to cope with them. Some of my patients have spent their lives struggling with an unhappy digestion. After three months of treatment one woman told me that she felt happy inside for the first time in her life. Since childhood she had been pasty-faced, bloated and always anxious. When she came to me she had a bad skin problem and was chronically constipated. It turned out that she had developed an 'intolerance' to wheat which had been fed by her family circumstances – her father was a baker. After 20 or so years of gradual deterioration many people that I treat no longer know what it means to wake up happy. They have got so used to feeling below par that they have no idea what it means to feel really well. When they put their digestion right, after working through one of my eating plans, I am as pleased as they are.

The treatment section of the book centres on three basic eating plans, with accompanying recipes, for those with the most common chronic digestive problems. This is followed by suggestions for keeping your store cupboard well stocked with gut-friendly ingredients, a selection of recipes for what I call 'maintainance meals', and, hopefully, a boon for busy mothers – ideas for feeding the young.

I want to show that it is possible to solve chronic difficulties with digestion and eventually go on to eat a delicious, broad range of foods. There is an extensive A–Z of foods (and herbs) at the back of the book to help you make wise choices when it comes to devising recipes for yourself. I have left it to you to use the advice and information on offer creatively, to suit your tastes and situation. Thinking about what you are eating and how you are eating may seem difficult and bothersome in the beginning, but if my patients are anything to go by, it will ultimately be a rewarding experience.

Some of the recipes included have been supplied by my patients. I hope their efforts will encourage you to try your hand at fashioning imaginative meals in the image of your digestion, using ingredients that suit it. Ultimately, *The Gut Reaction Eating Plan* is a movable feast – your feast.

Chapter One

THE FUNDAMENTALS OF
HEALTHY EATING

Before we can make sensible decisions about what to eat we need to understand what happens to food when it leaves our plate. The first principles of healthy eating relate to the gut, our in-built waste disposal unit and distributor of nutrients. An understanding of how the digestion works was a cornerstone of *Gut Reaction*. I will not go into the same detail here, but there are certain key factors about the digestion which need to be reiterated. Unless the intimate relationship between digestion and well-being are appreciated, the reasoning behind much of what follows later, especially the eating plans, will be lost on the reader.

No Mean Machine

Most people seem to regard the digestive system as something that has very little to do with them. It is like the lavatory – necessary but not the sort of thing we want to go into too deeply or ask questions about. However, unlike a lavatory or a car engine, it cannot be replaced successfully when something goes radically wrong with it. When it splutters to a halt, only loving restoration will do, and even this may not always do the trick.

The gut can be likened to the internal combustion engine, its various parts working together to propel us forward. One gut looks very much like another, and if we could look under our own bonnet and compare what is there with what is under our neighbour's bonnet, it is unlikely that we would notice any differences. The same would go for two new combustion engines. The quality of the components may vary – just as hereditary factors in humans may result in one part of the body being weaker or stronger – but only use over time will reveal the character of the engine and its efficiency. The engine that is routinely driven hard and fast or neglected and rarely serviced will need to be especially robust if it is not to break down. Another engine, perhaps one made of lower quality components, might give reliable service for years in the hands of a careful owner. The quality of the fuel put into the car is of secondary importance to the overall care. Just as the best grade fuel could not be expected to bring a clapped out engine to life, so nutrient-dense food will not revive a troubled digestive system. Such food is wasted when the system processing it is faulty through bad usage.

In order for food to benefit us we need to ensure that the gut is in good order. The first casualties of any problem with digestion are the beneficial bacterial microflora which reside in the lining of the gut. The most important of the 400 or so species of microflora is *Lactobacillus acidophilus*, which promotes digestion, detoxification (by the *Bifido* bacterium) and the absorption of nutrients. Other 'friendly' bacteria are involved in metabolising vitamins, synthesising saturated fatty acids and protecting us against germs. These bacterial flora are our buffer against disease, our insurance policy for a healthy future. There are other, so-called 'unfriendly', bacteria which are opportunistic and cause disease. In the individual whose digestive system is functioning well these bacteria are kept in check. However, when they are allowed to get the upper hand and outnumber the 'friendly' bacteria the general health of the body suffers. 'Unfriendly' bacteria thrive in toxic conditions and if they are allowed to flourish they will, like some aggressive super-state, invade neighbouring tissue and cause mayhem. The *Helicobacter pylori* bacterium, for example, an organism which has been identified as the principal culprit in a vast majority of cases of ulcerated or inflamed stomachs, releases a cytotoxin that can damage cells.

The wall of the gut should be regarded as our front line and 'friendly' bacteria its defenders. The wall has to be permeable in order to allow the active transport of nutrients. However, it must not become too permeable – or 'leaky' – with gaps developing between the cells, as happens when the gut is damaged. Think of your gut wall as a frontier with a few designated crossing places and the rest of it as an impregnable line. If those undesirable 'unfriendly' bacteria manage to breach the wall, toxins will pass into the bloodstream. At the same time malabsorption will occur, because of cell damage at the sites where nutrients are carried across the gut wall.

The most harmful aspect of poor absorption resulting from incorrect fermentation is that it forces the body to feed on itself. The body will try to make up for nutritional shortfalls by breaking down tissue. Unfortunately for the stomach the mucosal lining and muscle tissue are often the first casualties of this process: damaged in the first instance by the acidity which has produced malabsorption, it is then asset-stripped further by a body in desperate need of nourishment. The most important of the nutrients required by the body are the essential amino acids, the chemical units that make up proteins which go into our muscles, ligaments, organs, glands, nails, hair and most of our body fluids. If we are not able to absorb sufficient protein to build these units, numerous disorders may occur.

The extent and severity of the damage will depend on the individual's susceptibility to certain disease states and the strength of the immune system. So-called leaky gut syndrome is associated with a host of disorders, including food allergies such as asthma and eczema, inflammatory joint diseases, auto-immune diseases, chronic fatigue, fibromyalgia, septicaemia and irritable bowel syndrome.

If the cells in your gut are damaged, no amount of balanced eating or taking of vitamins and minerals will keep you healthy. The nutrients we need for good health have to be absorbed and if the mechanism by which this is done is undermined the body will eventually sicken. The damage must be repaired. This can be aided by certain foods, but it may also require additional assistance in the form of T glutamine, the principal fuel of the gut lining (see page 140).

Understanding the Mechanics

So what is responsible for creating the toxicity that can cause this damage? The short answer is, we are. The toxicity that gives rise to these 'unfriendly' bacteria is manufactured in the body as a consequence of our eating habits. Most people find it hard to believe that the food meant to nourish them and keep them alive should in effect be slowly poisoning them. The point is that it would not become toxic if we played our part in supporting the digestive system. The food we eat does not start its journey along the digestive tract with a 'Danger – toxic waste' tag attached to it. It is what we ourselves do to it – also what we omit to do, either through ignorance or wilful neglect – that makes it toxic.

For food truly to nourish us it has to be processed into a form the body can use. The salivary enzymes are the first of the chemical aids the body uses for the purposes of digestion. The act of chewing should then stimulate the release of more salivary enzymes which, in addition to beginning the process of breaking down fats and starches, should also alert the stomach. Here, what we have eaten should be churned and treated with more enzymes and hydrochloric acid to break down protein molecules, sterilise 'unfriendly' bacteria and aid the body's absorption of minerals and iron. The lion's share of digestion and absorption, however, takes place in the food's next port of call, the small intestine, where enzymes secreted by the pancreas, Crypts of Lieberkuhn and the liver set to work. The waste then travels on to the large intestine for elimination.

This whole complex process may seem like a miracle of nature, but it will not work efficiently if the body's acid-alkaline response to food is not activated at the outset. The transformation of food into usable matter should begin as soon as we scent, or see, what we are about to eat. When we are hungry and our senses are aroused by the thought of food, we salivate. Chewing creates more saliva and the more we chew the greater the cocoon of alkalinity which forms round the food. Most of us fail to do this adequately. Incompletely processed food drops into a stomach which is unprepared for its arrival and thus does not release hydrochloric acid. This has a knock-on effect further down the processing chain, because the acid-sensitive cells in the duodenum do not react as they should by sending a message to the pancreas to produce neutralising or alkali-forming enzymes.

Gastric acids play a crucial role in digestion and assimilation, particularly of proteins and minerals; without the right acid, iron cannot be absorbed from meat, for example. Proteins cannot be broken down if there is an insufficient flow of acid into the stomach and will ferment into toxic molecules. The gastric acids are also key in preventing the overgrowth of 'unfriendly' bacterial flora in the small intestine.

The role of acids in digestion is often misunderstood. The fact that in some people they seem to be a cause of discomfort signifies a problem with the gut lining, not with the acid. Many people mistakenly believe that an acid-forming food is the same as an acid food. The lemon is often labelled an acid fruit and perceived to be bad because of the effect it has on people. If the gut lining is not in good order – probably as a result of years of bad fermentation – lemon will seem too acid because it will irritate, as will many other foods. The lemon is, in fact, an alkali-forming food and a great digestive aid, but it is not an appropriate food for those whose guts are in need of repair. There are many more acid-forming foods than alkali-forming ones, and learning to cope with them is essential if we are to enjoy a broad diet. I will go into this in more detail in later chapters. For now, just be aware that the acids we should produce when we eat are our natural allies.

A second, inter-related, problem is over-eating. The stomach is reckoned to be about 30 cm (12in) deep and about 10 cm (4in) wide. An old Tibetan master who once taught me used a more telling measure – if the contents of my rice bowl exceeded what would fit into my two cupped hands, I was being greedy. The wise person aims to nourish the body without over-taxing it in the process. This means eating a sensible amount at each sitting. I advise my patients to take a rice bowl in their hands to enable them to gauge the correct amount before making up their meal. I know how easy it is to cheat or delude ourselves. I once had a friend who was a wonderful cook and a foodaholic. He would cook us delicious meals using large bowls and plates, so that it would look as though we were sticking to the rules. Of course, we would stuff ourselves and end up feeling like a couple of geese being fattened for foie gras.

Every inch of the digestive tract and the pockets of activity attached to it forms part of the process of digestion. If one area of this production line is not working, or is working below par, the effects will be felt. Try to imagine your gut as a vat of wine and yourself as the vintner. In wine-making getting the fermentation right is usually the most difficult part of the process. The same principle applies to your digestive tract – only one small thing need go awry for the whole system to become toxic. Get the fermentation right and you will be a medal winner as far as your digestive system is concerned, get it wrong and the entire contents will turn sour.

The Liver

One of our most hard-working body parts is the liver, our largest gland, which weighs about 1.8kg (4lb), and in terms of the digestion is the most important. Without the bile that it secretes, fats would not be broken down, fat-soluble vitamins (A, D, E, F and K) would not be properly absorbed or calcium assimilated, beta-carotene would not be converted to Vitamin A, and peristalsis would be less efficient. Nutrients such as iron and Vitamins A, B_{12} and D are extracted by the liver and stored so that we may use them to enable us to perform everyday activities and to cope in times of physical stress. The liver plays a major role in regulating blood sugar levels, by activating the thyroid hormone thyroxin, and breaking down hormones such as adrenaline, oestrogen and insulin after they have performed their respective functions. The liver is our in-built detoxification unit, and we rely upon it to eliminate the by-products – ammonia and urea – which eating animal proteins creates. In addition to cleansing us of metabolic waste, it processes drugs, alcohol, and chemical and insecticide residues, by combining them with substances that are less toxic.

With so much to do already it seems unfair to burden the liver further, but that is what most of us do when we over-eat, rely on processed foods and consume too much alcohol. The liver is a bit of a perfectionist and will always try to convert what we give it into something beneficial. Unfortunately, if what it is being given has no nutritional content, the body will become progressively depleted and the liver progressively damaged.

The Cinderella Problem

The third 'basic' that needs to be understood concerns the levels of sugar, or glucose, in the blood. Judging from my patients, it would seem to be a major contributory factor to illness. The stability of the blood sugar is crucial if our immune system is to work well and protect us. In low blood sugar types – or hypoglycaemics – the body temperature is one or two degrees lower than in those in whom the blood sugar is balanced, indicating that the immune system is not functioning properly.

When I tell people they are low blood sugar types, their initial reaction is 'Oh God, am I diabetic?' The short answer is 'No'. Hypoglycaemia is not the same as diabetes, although, if it is not checked, it may eventually lead to old-age diabetes with its associated disorders of high blood pressure and heart problems. Basically, hypoglycaemia is about the body's gluco-chemical response to the foods put into it.

In order for the blood sugar to remain even the foods consumed must not be broken down and absorbed too quickly. The faster and higher the blood sugar rises the more insulin will be released by the body to clear the bloodstream of the glucose and move it into the muscles where it is used as energy. The body does not store insulin, so each time a food or substance that induces high blood sugar is ingested, this hormone has to be manufactured.

If the body is constantly being asked to counteract the effects of high blood sugar – as occurs when highly refined carbohydrates or stimulants such as coffee are consumed – health problems will eventually develop, especially if non-essential fats feature heavily in the diet. These fats hinder the ability of insulin to clear the bloodstream. The body will strive to produce insulin until supplies dry up through sheer exhaustion. It is not a complete glutton for punishment, however, and will eventually present the bill for its efforts to its tormentor – you. Diabetes mellitus, or worse, is not a price worth paying. You can easily avoid the glucose level rising too quickly, even when you eat foods that are high on the glycaemic response index, by chewing and insalivating your food well. (The principal difficulty with low blood sugar is recognising when you are in its grip and realising that what you may be reading as signs of 'you-ness' are in fact part of a damaging pattern. See pages 2–3 for additional information.)

Absorbing the Basics

The fundamentals, or basics, of healthy eating are intimately connected, and through them the body is helped to achieve the correct acid-alkaline balance. Unless they are properly understood, the food we eat will not benefit us as it should.

Basic One

● Chew each mouthful of food 50 times. Inadequate chewing is one of the principal causes of bad fermentation. If you do not chew each mouthful of food sufficiently – 50 times – to stimulate the release of enzymes, digestion cannot begin. Regard yourself as a catalyst; without your input, digestion will not happen.

Basic Two

● Do not over-eat. What your body cannot cope with will cling to you as excess weight and your gut as potentially harmful matter. If the gut is persistently over-loaded, the liver will malfunction and not render toxic substances harmless before they enter the bloodstream.

Basic Three

● Pay attention to your blood sugar levels. Keep them as even as possible by feeding the body appropriately (see page 26) at regular intervals and taking care with your chewing. Saliva alkalises food and also slows the body's glucose response to it.

Chapter Two

INTO THE LOOKING GLASS

It takes very little practical experimentation to discover that what we eat is vital to our well-being. A good test of this proposition is to eat too much sweet, rich food and then gauge how you feel on the following day. People with severe digestive difficulties do not have to go to these lengths to feel the adverse effects of a poor choice of food.

The wife of one of my patients could not understand why he should be so depressed most of the time. During his worst spell he would be in pain and his stomach would blow up every time he ate. It would have taken a saint or a masochist to be a bundle of fun in his situation. However, partly through ignorance – and partly because of her basically unsympathetic nature – she would not believe that his diet was responsible for making him feel ill. We take for granted that too much alcohol can damage us, but cannot – or will not – accept that food can have precisely the same effect. Solids are no different from wine; both are foods in that they enter the body and have to be dealt with. If the 'friendly' bacterial flora in our gut are depleted and we do not chew our food properly, it is possible to feel just as hungover after eating too much bread and cheese or sugary foods as it is after drinking too much wine. Some people will feel below par after drinking three glasses of wine, with another person it may take two bottles for their systems to feel similarly 'degraded'. The same principle applies to food.

We are all different, we are all at different stages. Some people can cope with food or drink better than others. Much of what we are in terms of our health and susceptibilities is inherited; we owe to our families more than merely a name. It is sensible to be aware of possible genetic weaknesses so that we can take measures to combat them. We may not be successful, but trying is better than pretending they do not exist or believing that it is not possible to 'buck' our genetic inheritance. In some very rare cases, this is true, but for the vast majority of people their health and well-being lies in their hands. We do have choices in life, we can make a difference. I come from a family which has a history of old-age diabetes and the illnesses associated with it, such as heart attacks and irritated bowel. Some members of my family had such poor digestion that they could not even cope with the roughage presented by a grape skin. At a very early age I decided that I did not want to be part of this tradition. It was a very simple choice to make: I wanted to wake up as happy as a child, healthily full of mischief and ready for life. Food has played an enormous part in giving me the means to solve my fermentation problems. Vitamins, minerals and supplements have also helped, but to rely solely on them is to misunderstand the nature of the digestion. A common complaint from new patients is that they have changed their diet, spent a small fortune on bottled 'cures' and are no further forward. Fundamentally, good health comes from many sources, not least from the inside. If the body cannot absorb what it is being given it will not show signs of improvement.

Without a sound digestive system we run a real risk of being at the mercy of illness, the nature of which will probably be determined by our genetic blueprint. The gut should be regarded as the centre of our universe, our most precious bodily possession. The fact that it is not is attested to by the large numbers of people who have digestive difficulties. I will go into the whys and wherefores of this in the next chapter. For now, I want you to appreciate that it is for the sake of our gut – and thus for the sake of our health – that we need to develop a deeper understanding of food and our relationship with it.

When food is talked about it is generally in regard to how it tastes or whether it is good for us. For most people what is 'good' is what they like and tickles their taste buds. Those who look at food from a nutritional perspective make their choices on the basis of what they think is good for them, often regardless of taste. The vitamin and mineral content of food, how it is grown, will be of paramount importance. Week in week out they will gamely wade through piles of raw vegetables, fruit, pulses and grains in their eagerness to do the right thing by their bodies. Often they find their bodies wish they were rather less diligent, because this type of diet requires a very strong digestion.

I have a number of patients who have been vegetarian for years who come to me with problems which are due to how and what they are eating. The deficiency is not in the food itself, but in their ability to cope with it. If a food cannot be digested properly by an individual, it is bad for them. The same food may be easily digested by another person, in which case I would regard it as good. So, as a first step, we have to look at what we eat in terms of how well we can digest it. We must not be put off by the sly digs of those who could probably digest galvanised steel. No two digestions are exactly the same and we have to work towards what is right for ours and not worry about conforming to some notional norm.

With Friends Like These ...

In my experience many digestive problems have their roots in childhood. The most obvious early influence on the development of our palette is that of a parent. For example, the children of a parent with a sweet tooth are likely to be given foods which reflect the parent's preference. It is easy to accept too the notion of the overly protective parent whose attitude instils fear of the outside world, or of the puritanical parent who fosters a disgust of sex. Similarly, in a household where breaking wind or going to the toilet is regarded as a ghastly unmentionable, children are likely to grow up with an in-built sense of denial about matters that should be regarded as natural and wholesome.

I know of a young woman who used to cycle to a nearby hotel in order to use their lavatory because she could not bring herself to defecate under the same roof as her husband. He was not to blame for this, being a down-to-earth individual who would unashamedly do what came naturally to him. Her attitude was purely a product of her upbringing. Not surprisingly, her habit of holding on until she was in the 'right' place resulted in her becoming constipated.

Attitudes and states of minds can, and do, affect the digestion. The body will always try to respond to our wishes, and if we tell ourselves something, it will usually oblige. As was revealed in *Gut*

Reaction, the digestion is not merely a mass of connecting tubes and pouches. It has a brain – called the enteric nervous system – which is linked by a series of intricate nerve pathways to the brain in our head. The state we are in at any given time is not lost on our lower brain and our thoughts can affect it for good or ill. Experience has probably taught most of us that if we eat when we are upset, for example, indigestion is bound to result. The enteric system will, in effect, cry or get mad with us and be rendered useless in its role of organising the digestive process. In such ways do we unwittingly undermine our immune system.

When the digestion is put out of kilter by our actions it cannot be expected automatically to right itself and not bother us with the consequences. People who are prone to digestive problems have to be aware of themselves sufficiently to pre-empt problems. Bad fermentation does not result only from how much we eat. An identical meal can affect us differently depending on the state we are in: whether we are tired, angry or upset, or relaxed, contented and feeling good-humoured. When stress is allowed to take over, the stomach will react by blowing up. If you are aware of being in a stew about something – no matter how trivial – slow yourself down. Talk yourself into relaxing. It is never a good idea to take a problem with you to the dinner table in order to 'talk it out'. If this is unavoidable, however, choose your food very carefully. Certainly, avoid heavy proteins or shellfish – foods that require your enzymes to do their best work – in favour of fish, rice or vegetables. Eat less than you would normally and concentrate on chewing well. The more stressed you are the more careful you have to be with yourself.

The Nanny State

Some people are in the fortunate position of being able to suit themselves about how to spend their time, so for them the changes I shall be suggesting should not be difficult to incorporate. I am well aware, however, that a greater number are not in this situation, and for them the idea of preparing a snack mid-morning or afternoon is a luxury they can only dream about. A demanding job and nannying yourself do not go together. I have to get round this problem on a daily basis with my patients. Everybody's situation is different and you may find yourself having to compromise. If you do, take responsibility for this decision by expecting slower progress. The one area of the programme that you must not short-cut on is the diet. This is fundamental, whereas the supplements are adjuncts: desirable and helpful, but not vital.

Constant busyness is, of course, a principal cause of digestive problems, so in addition to adopting the diet plan the person whose time is under pressure must try to reduce the stress this can cause. If we are constantly doing, the digestion will be blocked, because the conditions are not right for it to do its job properly. The digestion starts going wrong the moment we gulp down that slice of toast before we rush off to catch the train in the morning. The cycle continues when we 'grab' a sandwich to eat between meetings or while we are bent over paperwork or a computer key-board. It does not end when we get home either, because by this time we are tired, and so is our digestion, but invariably we will give it the kind of meal it cannot cope with.

Even the most manically busy people must try to ring-fence meal times or at least concentrate on what will help their digestion while they eat. Imagine yourself releasing any tension you may be holding inside. Look upon the food you are eating as a great pleasure. Hold this feeling of pleasure while you are chewing. That thought will be transmitted to your gut where it will stimulate your natural helpers, those enzymes and stomach acids, into action. If it makes it any easier, devise a mantra to help you slip into 'meal mode'. Whatever the difficulties posed by your own set of circumstances, do what you can and persevere. Also do not be frightened of asking for assistance.

As a small child I used to keep trolls under my bed and when-ever I felt in need I would ask them for help. A Bedouin told me that in his culture the person in need would write down what he or she wanted to change and then burn the note while meditating on the idea of the universe sorting out the problem. Native Americans tear their written request into tiny pieces, then scatter them in a river with the injunction that the pieces should go to the source and come back with the answer. The fear of rejection prevents most of us from asking for help in our everyday lives. I encourage my patients to explore this idea and leave it to them to decide on a method of asking that is right for them. By asking, you are concentrating your thoughts on the desired result and not relying on some extraneous agent – for example, me – to be the sole determining factor of success or failure. You will gain in the long run.

An important part of my job is to help people think their way round problems – real or imagined – pertaining to their treatment. With some patients it can seem as though some aspect of themselves is intent on preventing recovery. One man with a potentially life-threatening viral condition started the regime I had devised, followed it precisely for about a fortnight, then stopped. The next time I saw him he said he had lost the medicines I had given him and that he had stopped taking one of the supplements because it tasted so ghastly. Given the fact that he said he had felt better while he was following the regime, I would have thought this was a discomfort worth enduring. Every suggestion I made for cutting the mixture down met with some objection. I suspect that his reason for prevaricating was based on a fear of losing control. In my experience people who are used to being in a dominant position – and this individual is a wealthy businessman – carry their need for control into all aspects of their lives, including their illnesses. For him, the idea that the treatment plan might be working posed a threat to his self-esteem. Like many powerful people, he is uncomfortable in situations where he is not the one pulling the strings and providing answers. Finding that we have a health problem which is not easily amenable to treatment can be a very unsettling experience. In such circumstances it is wise to ensure the ego does not work against us. Ultimately, if we want to get better we have to help ourselves, which means not making excuses, and getting on with the business of being treated.

The Blame Culture

Ignorance of how the body works leaves us open to making the wrong decisions. We can find ourselves looking to the wrong remedies for a 'solution' or 'cure'. Some people are born with an allergy programmed into their genes. In some of these cases eating a specific food – hazelnut, for example – will cause death because a specific gene is faulty. In others, too much of a particular food eaten in childhood may trigger an allergic response later in life. True food allergies are rare but to judge from the explosion of interest in so called 'exclusion diets' and allergy testing in recent years, one could be forgiven for thinking that we were witnessing an epidemic. What these figures reflect, in my opinion, is the vast number of people whose digestive systems are failing to cope with what is being put into them. Food allergies without a genetic component are associated with disease-causing agents, such as yeasts (*Candida albicans*) and allergenic food molecules, entering the bloodstream. In these cases taking out foods which are perceived to be causing the problem will normally only work for a short period. It is no coincidence that the foods most commonly excluded – such as wheat, cheese and dairy products – should be the most difficult for the digestion to process. If the lining of the gut is intact and the microflora in balance and your alkaline-acid response from the small intestine is alive, you are unlikely to develop a food intolerance which may seem like an allergy. If you have a food intolerance, you must set about rebuilding the damaged cells in the gut wall and regenerating the flora. The problem is with the state of the gut, not the foods you are eating.

It seems we are always looking for someone or something to blame when our health goes wrong. We prefer to feel we have been 'done to' rather than brought the problem on ourselves. If we want to be healthy, we must be prepared to get to know ourselves. Nobody – and certainly no machine – should know a body better than the individual inhabiting it. If you are in tune with your body and sensitive to its requirements, you should know what is suiting it and what is not. We humans are great ones for wishful thinking, burying our heads in the sand and passing any aggravating bucks to someone else for them to solve for us. At some point where our well-being is concerned, we have to be prepared to take responsibility and take action.

The Bottom Line

Honesty is particularly important where problems with the digestion are concerned. Take wind. It has a nasty knack of catching us at the most inauspicious – and sometimes hilarious – moments. A girlfriend confided how wind would often form when she was lying down, or sitting in the theatre or cinema. Her worst experience had been when she was with a lover. During a pause in coital proceedings she had become conscious of a compelling urge to break wind. Rather than relieve her discomfort openly, she played possum until she judged she could safely inch out of bed and make for a point downstairs, where, out of earshot, she could let out a king-sized report. The consequences of wind are regarded as purely social by the majority of us and never related to our health.

More distressing than funny was the case of a patient of mine, a ballet dancer, who was suffering so badly from wind that it would be released every time he lifted his partner or executed a jump. His worry about this situation was making performing an ordeal. I suspect that had his problem been of a different nature, he would have sought help sooner. But wind, like diarrhoea and incontinence, are taboo ailments; they are among the common disorders that dare not speak their names. The sufferers invariably think they are the only ones and that they are freaky, when in fact there are many others with exactly the same problem who are also enduring in silence.

Our social conditioning is such that it is simply not done to talk about certain bodily functions. One is expected to keep that sort of thing to oneself and if, through some lapse in self-control, one fails, you can rely on the people in the immediate vicinity to pretend they are deaf or have a blocked nose. This conspiracy of silence only serves to reinforce many of the problems associated with poor digestion. Farting, belching and diarrhoea may not be perceived as 'nice', but they are facts of life. So, if you are one of those shrinking flowers, try not to be. Look squarely at whatever your problem is and promise it a solution.

Chapter Three

WHAT'S EATING YOU?

Most people do not think about their digestion until it starts to demand their attention and even then they will often choose to ignore or mask the problem rather than treat it as a warning sign. If they seek help and no underlying clinical condition is revealed, they will probably be sent away with the loose injunction to mind what they eat. Unfortunately, unless the root causes of poor digestion are tackled, the sufferer will eventually find that he or she is unable to eat anything without the gut complaining loudly and painfully.

Healthy eating is not merely a question of choosing foods that received opinion says are good for us. We have to know where we are in terms of our health in order to choose wisely. A sure-fire way of finding out is to examine how well we are digesting our food.

Indigestion

The clinical definition of indigestion relates the problem specifically to the stomach, although the effects of not digesting properly are to be seen and felt throughout the body. Indigestion signifies that we are not coping with the food we are eating. You have only to look at people's bodies to see whose system is coping and whose is not. Excess weight indicates undigested food, as do wind and constipation.

The first sign of indigestion – belching – is usually more obvious in men, many of whom will not think twice about releasing wind in public. Women are far more susceptible to ideas of what constitutes good manners and will tend to swallow their discomfort rather than openly expel the air billowing inside them. Sufferers from indigestion, of both sexes, tend to say that something has 'disagreed' with them, unfairly placing the onus on the food consumed. By making a joke of it, we reduce the significance of indigestion, dismissing it as we might a particularly violent sneeze. The inference is that there is no harm in a puff of wind or a discreet belch. Everybody does it. Everybody might, but it is interesting how many people try to pretend they do not and for reasons which have nothing to do with health. A puff of intestinal wind is never harmless. It is a signal that something is amiss which needs to be put right if it is not to lead to greater problems.

Once we settle into a routine with indigestion, it is liable to progress and cause serious problems with our health, especially in middle age when our ability to deal with food declines naturally as the body reduces production of the digestive enzymes that break down what we eat.

Wind

The short-term consequence of eating food that we have difficulty digesting is pain or discomfort in the form of wind. Depending on your disposition and upbringing, wind is a fascinating mystery, an unspeakable embarrassment, a joke or something to be expected, like rain at Wimbledon. It is something that seems to happen spontaneously and, if we are unfortunate and especially coy about this universally shared phenomenon, all too often publicly. The first thing that needs to be said about wind is that we are responsible for its creation and cannot with a clear conscience blame it on what we have eaten. Some foods are undoubtedly more wind-forming than others, but this should be taken into account when they are eaten, by ensuring that they are chewed very thoroughly. If the digestion is in a particularly explosive and gassy state, then they should be avoided until the system has calmed down enough to cope with them; there is little point in distressing the body unnecessarily. It is wise to learn which foods your body objects to and respect its wishes until you have learnt how to cope.

Inherent indigestibility, however, is not the principal factor in the buildup of wind and cannot be blamed for the loud reports which follow meals made from innocuous ingredients. A sweetly functioning digestive system should deal with these without a ripple of protest. Wind which makes itself felt at either end of the body signifies a buildup of undigested matter in the system. The only difference between a belch and a fart is that they indicate faulty digestion at opposite ends of the digestive tract.

The classic wind sufferer is caught in an unpleasant cycle of one incompletely digested meal following another into the system. Imagine, day after day, breakfast, lunch and dinner dropping onto one another before the previous offering has been coped with. Often the stomachs of wind sufferers will 'grow' during the day and only begin to regain their normal size during the night when sleep prevents further eating and thus greater expansion.

The windy gut will give off distress signals before it erupts, usually gurgling and distending as the body's enzymes struggle to deal with the over-capacity. Wind is the body's way of telling you that it is being overwhelmed by superior forces. Tactical retreat is usually called for.

One bad thing usually leads to another where the digestion is concerned, unless the first signs of disquiet are taken seriously. The windy individual who regularly over-eats will be constipated and may go on to develop an irritated bowel.

The Bermuda Triangle: Constipation, Diarrhoea and Irritated Bowel

Many people suffer with constipation without realising it, accepting as perfectly 'normal' that their bowels do not open more than once in two days or longer. Normal is not the same as healthy, however. The properly functioning bowel should open twice a day.

There are several reasons for constipation. An insufficient intake of water and fibre is the most common cause. The colon requires a minimum of a litre and a half of water each day to help it process waste efficiently and speedily; it also requires sufficient fibre to assist transit by creating bulk in the stool.

Not responding to the bowel's prompting to empty it is a less talked about, but common cause of constipation. We may not be in the 'right place' and so we will hold on. If we get into the habit of holding on and putting off evacuation, the bowel adjusts to the situation and becomes sluggish. Imagine asking someone out who consistently declines your invitations. Eventually you stop asking. It is a similar situation with the bowel which, after several refusals, will make other arrangements. These arrangements are not to your benefit and at the earliest opportunity the bowel should be coaxed back into performing as it should.

We take for granted that small children have to be potty trained. Potty training is like learning the alphabet – it is a foundation stone – but as we get older we tend to forget its importance and its purpose. Being 'regular' can be as much about maintaining a line of communication with the bowel as having an appropriate diet. Adhering to the principle of regularity and responding to the urge to defecate whenever it arises is the same whether we are five or 50. Too often, though, we become less comfortable with doing what should come naturally and are easily inhibited.

Another form of blocking that causes constipation occurs in stressed, tense individuals, often low blood sugar types (see pages 21–3). Typically food is eaten in a rush, not chewed properly and when it enters the stomach the right digestive juices will not have been released to deal with it: gastric acid and pepsin will not be excreted in sufficient quantities and the transformations that have to occur in the duodenum – assisted by pancreatic enzymes and bile – will not be completed. If food is not digested it cannot be eliminated from the system. In people in whom constipation is chronic, undigested matter adheres to the wall of the bowel as this erodes and becomes sticky with the decline in health of the microflora, and a log-jam develops.

Diarrhoea is the body's way of getting rid of substances that are irritating the gut wall. This might be a short-term irritation; for example, in food poisoning. In many people, however, diarrhoea is ever present, as a component of what is known as irritable bowel syndrome (IBS). Indigestion – constipation – diarrhoea – irritated bowel. For many people there is an inevitability about this linkage; certainly these conditions are intimately associated. This is how the pattern develops: indigestion leads to constipation which in time will lead to irritation of the gut wall. The body will try to protect the gut tissue by releasing water, as it would if you burnt yourself, withdrawing fluid from uninjured areas of the body and sending it to the site of the injury.

Irritated bowel means food is collecting in a sluggish gut that is only processing waste every three or four days, by which time the gut is so toxic that faeces have to be literally shot out of the system to minimize further damage. Some people with IBS experience one week of constipation followed by one week of diarrhoea.

Fundamentally, the IBS sufferer is constipated, but when the gut becomes toxic enough the body will take its own measures to throw out the undigested matter in the gut. If this state of affairs is allowed to continue, the condition of the gut will deteriorate further, with inflammation resulting in diverticulitis and colitis.

Low Blood Sugar

Many people suffer with their digestion because they are low blood sugar (LBS) types. Balanced blood sugar and sound digestion go hand-in-hand with good health. I have already explained at some length what happens chemically when low blood sugar occurs (see page 7). Here we will look at the effect these chemical changes have on the sufferer.

Many people suffer from low blood sugar without realising it, and the first hurdle is to acknowledge membership of this vast – and growing – club. I always refer to people who suffer from low blood sugar as a type because their behaviour tends to fit a pattern.

Some people can eat three meals a day, and maintain concentration well between these fuel stops without craving for that 'little something'. These people are not LBS sufferers. Nor are the people who eat virtually nothing, smoke and drink as though there is no tomorrow and end up burying all their peers. They are the jokers in the pack of life, the ones on whom health myths are based. The classic LBS type has a love-hate relationship with food. Nobody likes to be so dependent that every two or three hours they have to go in search of sustenance in order to stop their brain scrambling. They are the ones in whom an in-built 'I've had enough' switch seems to be absent and who are usually incapable of resisting that drink, nibble, or cigarette too far. This may with like plain greed but rather it is a neediness, as though the body knows there is a deficiency which it is trying to get the sufferer to rectify.

When LBS types short-fuse or become tearful for no apparent reason, they are not being merely temperamental or auditioning for membership of the awkward squad. These are signs that blood sugar levels are plummeting and the body is in the nutritional equivalent of a nose-dive. The message is 'Mayday. Crash imminent due to lack of appropriate grade fuel.' Unfortunately, the means by which the LBS type usually chooses to avert this disaster is the least appropriate. LBS types have a weakness for the foods that they would do well to avoid – carbohydrates – which, together with caffeine and nicotine, are the worst offenders in respect of raising blood sugar levels. These go straight into the bloodstream in double-quick time, providing a short-term boost in energy, but one akin to the stimulus characteristic of some drugs, producing a high followed by an unpleasant down. The more frequently they are relied upon to deliver the lift the body is craving, the wider and higher the swings in blood sugar levels will go. Short-term foods produce short-term results and those who resort to them are always hungry.

There is another variation on a theme of the LBS type which deserves a mention. This one will tend to be a self-denier of sorts, who, in the course of over-achieving and determining to keep up with the whirligig of a life he or she has created, will refuse most of the body's entreaties for genuine sustenance. Toughing it out is the worst course of action for the low blood sugar type, and even people who did not start life as LBS types may become them if they follow this regime. In the good health stakes, medals are not awarded for repeatedly crashing through some notional pain barrier. Unfortunately, some people become addicted to this way of living and perhaps the image of the 'achiever' – strong black coffee and cigarettes throughout the day, maybe a sandwich snatched half-way through the afternoon, working late and getting home to 'relax' with a bottle of wine and a takeaway. The striving may be part of some deeper insecurity, perhaps a way of proving that they are worthy of admiration or love.

At this point you are probably resisting the idea of being labelled LBS. Everyone is allowed to get hungry, aren't they? Anyway, you never – or rarely – eat 'junk' food, with all those added sugars, fats and deadly E-numbers. You don't even have a sweet tooth. You eat only 'good' carbohydrates – i.e. foods such as pasta, wholemeal bread, potatoes. Everyone says they are good for you. Don't they? If you look at them in terms of the vitamins and minerals they contain, the answer is 'Yes'. The problem with looking at them purely in this way is that it takes no account of how your body is responding to them.

Every food we eat registers a glycaemic response in our body. Some foods elicit a high glycaemic response, with sugar, not surprisingly, eliciting the highest. Others elicit a low or lower gly-caemic response. The degree to which the blood sugar rises when carbohydrates are ingested will depend on how quickly they enter the bloodstream. This relates directly back to the earlier discussion about chewing – thorough chewing ensures that the chemical trans-formation of food is both complete and orderly, with the saliva enveloping each mouthful of food, buffering the body against a fast glucose response. A gobbled carbohydrate may be imagined as a sort of gate-crasher, compelling its way into the bloodstream in an unseemly manner and forcing the body to manufacture more insulin than is good for it. If the food in question is a wholefood, thorough chewing could have transformed it into a quiet, well-mannered vis-itor to your digestive tract. Or could it? Potatoes are nutritionally good but, depending on how you cook them, they can elicit very different responses. In the low blood sugar person mashed potatoes will slide down into the gut as rapidly as any junk food and elicit a high glycaemic response, whereas if they are cooked in their skins, and thus have to be chewed, the response will be greatly reduced. Transforming 'junk' carbohydrates, such as crisps and other highly refined foods, is very difficult; because they are so finely ground, they hit the bloodstream virtually as soon as they are swallowed. However, even their potentially negative impact can be partially ameliorated by thorough chewing. The low blood sugar person should be very careful about the carbohydrates he or she consumes and take measures to ensure they are made as digestible as possible.

Most LBS types are forced to confront themselves before they arrive prematurely at the Pearly Gates, because theirs is an unsus-tainable position. In my experience, they are the ones who most quickly get into trouble with their health. The pity is that low blood sugar is easily managed and need not be allowed to develop into less tractable problems. If you are still not convinced you are a low blood sugar type, complete the following test.

Drink a glass of red wine on an empty stomach and monitor its effects:

- Did you feel groggy or slightly tipsy?
- Did you experience a 'high' followed by a 'low'?
- Did you want another glass, then another . . . ?

If the answer to any of these is 'Yes', you are 100 per cent LBS. Welcome to the club!

Chapter Four

THE EATING PLANS

Most people who come to me are floundering at some point in the Bermuda Triangle of constipation, diarrhoea and irritated bowel. These three basic digestive difficulties provide the seed ground for illness. Invariably patients will come with what is to them a totally unconnected problem – perhaps blotchy skin, headaches, respiratory problems, swollen legs or aches and pains. And, invariably, as soon as the digestion is righted, by slowly changing the fermentation, these symptoms subside and the patient feels better.

Needless to say, the following eating plans are basic in that they do not take into account the additional recommendations I would make in specific cases. No two digestions are identical and individual weak points have to be taken into account when I see patients on a one-to-one basis. However, the plans should provide enough guidance to enable you to improve the health of your gut so that you are then able to eat normally. I have provided a selection of Maintenance Recipes (pages 72–94) to help you when you reach this stage.

The plans should not become a strait-jacket; they should be a springboard to better, tastier things. A danger with many diets is that perfectly good foods are renounced forever. This is not my way – it is necessary only to cut out completely what your gut cannot cope with when it is well. So, treat the plans as a first phase.

Before we get to that first phase, I want to anticipate some of the 'whys' that are bound to form in your head when you start working with the plans.

Repairing the Damage

The diets I devise are based on the principle of assessing the degree of degradation of the mucosal lining of the gut and rectifying this damage. The tiny delicate hairs (villi) embedded in the gut lining are usually the first casualties of a digestion in distress. Absorption is hindered if these hairs become clogged with undigested matter. Iron, for example, is vital to the maintenance of good health and cannot be absorbed if the digestion is poor. People who do not produce enough hydrochloric acid – most constipation sufferers fit this category – are nearly always deficient in iron because their bodies are not able to break down protein. Eating even larger amounts of protein is not the answer. The only sure remedy is to assist the body's ability to absorb, by ensuring that two-thirds of the volume of each meal is composed of vegetables and that the shortfall in hydrochloric acid is rectified.

Restoring the bacterial flora that populate the lining of the gut and colon must be done slowly. At least 85 per cent of the bacteria in the colon should be of the *Lactobacillus* type. In most people, however, it is the 'unfriendly' coliform bacteria which achieves this percentage. The result of this imbalance is excessive flatulence, bloating, toxicity, constipation and malabsorption. Bringing the bacterial flora back into balance means making the body more alkaline so that it does not provide the rich pickings that are available to harmful agents in a toxic or acid system, leading to serious illness.

Supplements can speed the process of repair. Acidophilus used in conjunction with digestive enzymes helps to remedy any imbalance. Where there is evidence of malabsorption (such as in cases of chronic diarrhoea), I will include in the eating plan an amino acid called L-glutamine, which also contains a constituent dedicated to detoxification. The use of both Acidophilus and L-glutamine requires patience and sensitivity on the part of the person being treated. Dosages cannot be fixed precisely, especially in the initial stages of treatment, and patients must learn to 'feel' their way and be prepared to take tiny amounts. The aim of treatment is to restore the bacterial balance gradually, without provoking an adverse reaction, which can easily occur if these supplements are taken too liberally.

Important though these supplements are, it is important not to fall into the trap of believing that they alone will do the trick. Our choice of food is fundamental to the healing process, and, if we learn to get it right, it alone will ensure that the gut remains in good order.

People with perfect digestion do not experience dips in their blood sugar levels, nor do they have the urge to over-indulge. They can eat whatever they like because their food is digested along the length of the digestive tract. The many of us who are not so blessed have to remind ourselves not to eat too much and not to gobble our food. We also have to learn to discriminate between foods.

Generally, the foods that do us most good are nutritionally dense, digestible and do not rapidly break down into simple sugars. As I explained in the section on low blood sugar (see pages 21–3), foods which elicit a high glycaemic response, sending our blood sugar levels soaring, are to be avoided, because they overwork the digestive system and short-change us nutritionally. The more slowly a food is digested the longer the supply of energy and, providing the gut is in good condition, the more complete the take-up of nutrients by the body.

The foods with the highest glucose response are finely ground carbohydrates or starches. Obviously, not all carbohydrates are 'bad' in this way; we have to learn to differentiate. As a general rule I ask people to eliminate from their diet only the foods which cannot be chewed well enough to transform them. It is, for example, incredibly difficult to slow the rate at which foods such as potatoes (especially mashed potatoes) or bread are absorbed and hit the bloodstream. The gluten in wheat poses difficulties for most people in whom the fermentation is not right, by continuing to ferment in the gut. Foods which are amenable to transformation with a bit of jaw power can be re-introduced at a later stage, when the digestion is stronger and the fermentation has changed.

Combining our foods wisely – by not eating proteins and starches at the same meal – is another golden rule for the middle-aged and badly fermenting person, in whom the production of digestive enzymes is markedly declining. Starch and proteins require the body to make different enzymes for their digestion, and when supplies of these enzymes are in short supply, it is far less wearing (and painful) if the digestive system is allowed to process them separately. Serving potatoes, pasta or rice with meat or fish is guaranteed to force your gut to work over-time and give you that uncomfortable 'brick in the stomach' experience.

If we chew well, eat lightly (and not at all when we are stressed or over-tired) and do not mix starches and proteins, the body will show its gratitude. If we pay attention to how we eat our food, we greatly reduce the likelihood of its turning acid when it gets inside us.

Changing the Culture

In our designer-conscious age we tend to pay more attention to how food looks than what can be done with it. Foods that are difficult to digest can be rendered less harmful, even positively benign, by the way we treat them. Where food is concerned there is little that our distant ancestors could not teach us; they learnt by sheer trial and error and much of the wisdom we tend to dismiss as folklore has sound reasoning behind it. People were once aware of the relationships between certain foods. With our modern reliance on and preoccupation with ready-made meals, this understanding has been lost. We have forgotten how to use our natural allies – herbs, for example – to keep the digestion sound and ourselves well. We can learn from the food traditions of other nations too. I encourage my patients to take what they require for good health from every available source.

When we digest food properly and subsequently eliminate it without delay, it does not get a chance to harm us. Some foods tend to leave an acid deposit in the gut. Meat, especially red meat, requires a lot of hydrochloric acid and pepsin to break it down.

People in the industrialised world have become used to eating far too much animal protein. Nutritional experts estimate that the body requires very little protein each day and cannot cope with more than 75 g (3 oz) at a time. No self-respecting steak-house would dream of serving up less than a quarter-pounder to its customers and then would probably regard it as a child or small eater's portion. We need to get away from thinking of animal protein as the most important item on our dinner plate. Unfortunately this has become ingrained in us after centuries of recipe making in which protein has been the focus, with the vegetables in attendance as a sort of supporting act. For the sake of our digestion this thinking needs to change. At any meal where protein or starch is eaten, vegetables and fruit should always be in a 3:1 majority, to help neutralise the acid tendency of these foods.

The cultures with the healthiest diets have devised ways of aiding the digestion where animal proteins are concerned. The Italians and Greeks have for centuries used olive oil and lemon as condiments for protein dishes. The oil triggers the liver to release more bile and keeps the metabolic rate high, while the acidity of the lemon performs the task of the hydrochloric acid (breaking down the fibres in the meat) as well as stimulating the release of pancreatic juices. In Iranian and Middle Eastern cookery red meat is invariably stewed very slowly with dried lime and alkali-forming herbs. The meat emerges at the end of this process succulent, tender, intensely flavoured and virtually pre-digested. People who find red meat constipating should try this method – as well as eat a bit less of it.

Sauerkraut is not everyone's idea of a great dish but it serves a very valuable purpose, helping to break down proteins by changing the acidity in the gut. The benefits of sauerkraut derive from the lactic acid which the fermenting cabbage, onions, herbs and seasonings produce. Lactic acid fermentations promote the health and growth of 'friendly' bacterial flora at the expense of harmful micro-organisms in the gut by regulating the secretion of gastric acid and stimulating the pancreas; see Molkosan under Supplements (page 142). Far Eastern cultures have used lactic fermentations for centuries: the Umeboshi plum and pickled condiments used by the Japanese in their cooking are examples. In my own country, Sweden, we have a range of alcoholic bitters, similar to Schnapps, which were not originally devised to help people get drunk but to aid their digestion.

These beneficial fermentations come in various forms, so if one kind does not suit you, it should be possible to find another that does. If you find raw sauerkraut difficult to take, try sauerkraut juice or whey concentrate, or the other fermented foods I have already mentioned. Sauerkraut can be bought either as a juice or the proper food, but beware of highly salted supermarket brands.

There are many more common ingredients which we can use to act as a foil for foods that tend to make us acid or give a high glycaemic response. The first foil is our own digestive juices. Always sit down to a meal hungry and, if it is a heavy meal, accompany it with appetite sharpeners such as rocket, watercress, mustard and horseradish. An appetite that is put on its mettle will be far better able to deal with whatever is consumed.

Vegetables can cause digestive problems in sensitive stomachs. Certainly the much-vaunted virtues of raw vegetables only benefit people with a sound digestion. Light steaming renders them more digestible by starting the process of breaking down the cell walls. If you use this method, retain the cooking water, which is where most of the minerals from the vegetables will be, for use in soups. I like to stir-steam vegetables in stock and herbs, which ensures that most of the goodness is retained.

However, no matter how careful or loving the preparation of our chosen ingredients, never forget that we cannot buck the basics:

- If you over-eat, your digestion will suffer. Remember the cupped-hands rule (see page 5).
- If you do not chew your food, your digestion will suffer.
- If you allow the blood sugar level to dip, your digestion will suffer.
- If you are stressed or over-tired when you eat, your digestion will suffer.

Ignoring these facts will leave us no further forward. What we eat and how we eat come as a package where our digestion is concerned. This is probably the most difficult lesson for anyone who follows my eating plans to learn.

Food for Thought

Over-eating and not chewing our food are related tendencies. They are also very difficult for us to gauge. Many of us react to being hungry as we do to having an itch – we satisfy the sensation without thinking, and we eat until we are no longer hungry. Rarely do we set ourselves a limit; we just know when enough is enough. But over-eating can become a habit.

The idea of being restricted to the amount that will fill your two cupped hands may seem miserly, bordering on cruelty, especially at the end of a long, hard day when you are craving some sort of comfort. Hands, however, are usually a good indication of the physical frame nature has given you, so do not think what I am suggesting constitutes starvation rations. The old saying 'His eyes were bigger than his belly' suggests that the tendency to greed has been around for a very long time and is to be found in most of us.

If your hunger is not being satisfied, you need to look more closely at how you are eating. Chewing thoroughly is not only vital to breaking down the food to enable the digestive enzymes and stomach acid to process it efficiently, it leaves us with an accurate record of how much we have eaten. Usually what happens during a meal is that each mouthful of food is chewed perhaps half a dozen times before it is dumped into the next part of the digestive tract. If the food in question is soft, we tend to let it slide down without bothering to chew at all. When we chew so little it is no wonder we are left feeling hungry; we have not engaged with the food in any sense. Chewing properly is both a physical and sensory experience in which specific muscles and sense organs come into play. Eaten properly, each meal leaves a trace, even when it has been unmemorable or mundane. It is like going for a stroll and taking note of what you see and hear around you as opposed to rushing heedlessly from point A to point B.

The habit of 'bolting' is not usually troublesome when we are young and the body has a full complement of enzymes and acids to deal with what we ingest. However, in middle age, when the body begins to reduce its production of enzymes, unless we are very lucky the digestion will start to complain at such treatment and remind us of its existence. Middle age is also a time of opportunity. Once the arrogant certainties of youth are behind us we can start taking the digestion seriously. This means taking feeding seriously. Play a game with yourself that you might play with a child. When you give a child a sweet, it is advisable to tell the child that it will only get one, so that one should be savoured and made to last. If you make what you are eating last, it will seem more substantial and stay with you longer. When we chew, thoroughly, every meal can seem like a banquet; indeed, you will probably find the exercise quite tiring. To begin with, you may find it a bit of a chore, not to say boring, but this should not be an insuperable problem if you also take the opportunity to reassess your attitude to food.

Being the creatures that we are, it is very difficult for most of us to think about nothing while we are eating. One of the reasons that some people eat so quickly is because they regard eating time as 'dead' time – they would rather be doing something else. Ensure that you give yourself time to linger over your food. Take that time to think – not about your job, your relationships or the hundred and one things you have got to do during the day, but about the plate of food in front of you.

Make each chew a discovery. With each bite, ask yourself what the food tastes of. Describe it, and then describe the subsequent flavours that come into your mind as you continue to eat. You will find that many foods you take for granted and think you know will surprise you; even a solitary grape has hidden depths. Chew one very slowly and you will find that its flavour will change in your mouth. Foods which you may well previously have characterised as bland become sweet if they are allowed to unfold. When you eat properly, food reveals all of itself.

Savouring food teaches us to live in the moment and not always be rushing ahead of ourselves. We tend to expend far too much energy on worrying or thinking about what is around the corner. Even when we are in relaxed mode at the table we will tend to think of the next course while we are chomping our way through the preceding one. This is most noticeable with 'pudding people', for whom the ideal meal would probably consist of a succession of desserts. Faulty child psychology has encouraged this end-gaining. I wonder how many times since man discovered fire have reluctant children been threatened with – 'If you don't eat your greens, you won't get any pudding'. This attitude is programming children to shovel in food without any proper regard for it. We need to return food, its preparation and the eating of it to a central place in our hearts and minds. Food is one of the fundamentals of existence, as crucial as the air we breathe. If we honour its importance in practical ways, it will help to keep us healthy and truly be a life-giver.

Finally, I cannot over-emphasise the importance of 'listening' to your body. This takes practice but it is vital to getting the gut in tune. Being well is never just about what we eat. The gut suffers when we try to out-run our capacity. I know this from my own experience and that of my patients. Most of us need something to help us slow down. Regular exercise or bodywork will help to dissipate the many anxieties and stresses that are at the root of digestive problems. It is up to you to decide which form of mind/body work-out would suit you best: aromatherapy massage, flotation therapy, cranial osteopathy, Pilates and yoga are common and effective ways of helping us unwind and get back in balance with our true selves. Competitive and punishing sports can actually pile on the stress, so avoid them. We need a bit of kindness on an ongoing basis. When you are relaxed and in charge of your life, your gut will echo your well-being.

Constipation Eating Plan

Constipation signifies that undigested matter is in the intestinal tract as a result of the digestion being blocked. The cause might be over-eating, anxiety, a diet high in saturated animal fats and highly refined foods, especially carbohydrates, or a combination of these factors. Very few people know what constipation is and, if my experience is any guide, they will resist being categorised as constipated. Why is the idea of constipation so demeaning to our self-esteem? I suppose it conjures up childhood memories of sitting endlessly on a potty or having our noses held while spoonfuls of syrup of figs were poured down our throats. As adults we are past all that. We want our illnesses to be taken seriously, and treated seriously.

The first of the series of questions I put to patients during a consultation is 'Are you constipated?' They will invariably respond defensively and, significantly, non-specifically – 'Not more than the next person', is a common reply. I remember one elderly widower who had throughout his life 'gone' every four days. He was, he insisted, 'very regular'. I explained that I would like it to be more regular and that twice a day would be our goal. He had come to me complaining of tiredness which he was inclined to put down to his age. Constipation will tire the body by weighing it down with the toxic waste it should be eliminating.

After a few weeks of sticking to the regime I had worked out for him he began to realise just how much energy he had been lacking. He started eliminating twice a day and having 'floaters' as a matter of course. He experienced 'bright' days when nothing was a chore and he felt light in himself. It was as though he had re-discovered his life force. One day he told me, with a twinkle, that something was also 'waking up below'. Eventually he remarried and is now happy and still full of that life force. His case is a perfect illustration of the energy that is available to us all when we are fully well. Too often, it is assumed that the advancing years automatically bring a diminution in sexual energy and that wishing to have the energy to enjoy sex at this point in the game of life is a forlorn – and rather pitiable – hope. Not so. Energy is energy and if you are tired – no matter whether you are 30 or 70 – you will not feel like having sex.

Action Points

Before you look at the basic plan for constipation I want to explain its whys and wherefores and reiterate a few points I have already made.

- In most constipated people the pancreas is not getting a message from the duodenum to produce sufficient enzymes to break down either starch or protein. This is not the fault of either party but yours for not setting the digestive process in motion. Although I will be advising you to take a digestive enzyme, chewing well is still important.
- As a general rule you should avoid any foods that tend to be 'binding', such as eggs (especially hard-boiled), cheese, refined grains or cereals and potatoes. None of these foods is included in the recipes I have formulated for you.
- Generally, good vegetables for the constipation sufferer include carrots (raw or slightly cooked), celery, and bitter salad stuffs (such as rocket, chicory and watercress) which stimulate digestion. The cruciferous vegetables – broccoli, cabbage (cooked, perhaps with fennel; but even then they may be too wind-forming), spring greens (cooked) and spinach may also be tried. Whole green beans (runner beans or French) are delicious slightly cooked and then chopped into salads or served on their own with olive oil and cider vinegar.
- I have included some recipes which use red meat, but resist the temptation to eat too much of it. Remember, it is acid-forming and your body has to work hard to digest it. Do not make your body have to work too hard.

• Constipated people never drink enough water, which is vital if they are to become unconstipated. The large intestine requires roughly one and a half litres a day to help the process of peristalsis and prevent stools being hard and uncomfortable. Not all waters are the same and so it helps to know the differences between the best water – Natural Mineral Water – and the rest. See pages 128–9 for details. Drinking adequate amounts of water also ensures that any impurities are flushed from the system. The constipated person should drink twice the daily requirement.

Many people worry that if they have to drink so much more they will be condemned to trailing backwards and forwards to the lavatory, especially during the night. Men are very sensitive to this because of what they think it might reveal to wives or girlfriends about a totally unrelated aspect of their genitalia. This should not be an issue between lovers who are open with each other and supportive. Drinking more water will put the bladder under pressure temporarily, but it will soon adapt and strengthen to cope with the increase.

• The metabolic rate has to be kept up – mid-morning and mid-afternoon are particular danger spots in the day – to ensure that you do not run on nervous energy and block off the digestion further. This is a real danger with constipated people, who tend to be low blood sugar and thus rather tense, anxious types. (Read the sections on this under-reported phenomenon to see whether you fit the description – see pages 7–8 and 21–3). Their energy tends to be focused on survival and rarely will they give themselves time to relax, even when they get the chance. When the metabolic rate slows down, so does the digestion.

It is important for the low blood sugar constipation sufferer to have warm drinks throughout the day to help the gut remain relaxed and responsive. Cold drinks tend to make the digestive system tense and stop it functioning well. If you are aware of such tension, ease the situation by placing a hot water bottle on your stomach or at your back. This is the reason for feeding the body mid-morning and mid-afternoon – see Plan.

• The digestion has to be aided in a number of ways in the beginning to get the right acidity in the gut; essentially, it is this imbalance in acidity that is responsible for constipation. Enzymes (see page 139) should be taken at lunch and dinner to ensure that food is digested, especially proteins. Proceed slowly with this and be prepared to monitor yourself. I start patients off with Udo's Digestive Enzyme, supplemented by Udo's Super-5, then after 1–2 months substitute Gut Reaction Probion (see page 138) for the Super-5.

- Try to get into the habit of chewing herbs before you begin your meal. These will help to get your system ready to receive the food you are about to give it and should increase your own expectation of what you are about to receive. Fresh rosemary leaves, thyme, tarragon or fennel seeds should do the trick. The idea is not to eat masses of them – just a few leaves or seeds are needed to pep up the digestion.

Plan

Remember to drink at least 1.8 litres (about 8 glasses) of water – preferably Natural Mineral Water – in addition to other fluids daily.

On waking
A. Drink two glasses of water (taken from your daily 8 glasses) with a squeeze of natural lemon juice.
B. Lemon and olive oil drink (see page 48); this is preferable to Option A because the olive oil triggers the gall bladder, waking up the digestive system.

Breakfast
A. One green apple, grated, with oatbran porridge (see page 49) topped with a couple of tablespoons of yoghurt.
B. Kiwi fruit and papaya salad.
C. Although not ideal, if you feel that you need a more substantial breakfast, try organic sausages with tomato and mushrooms; grill all the ingredients; if tomatoes usually give you indigestion, exclude them.

Remember to eat some raw grated or stewed apple before your cooked breakfast or take a fibre drink after it.

After breakfast

A fibre drink (if not already taken): fruit juice with Oligo-fibre (see page 140); alternatively, you could incorporate the fibre with your breakfast by mixing some soaked linseed with any of the fruit components.

Mid-morning

A. Herb tea; whichever flavours you like – look at the herbs which are appropriate for constipation (see pages 131–7) and experiment. There are so many to choose from that to limit yourself to one or two types would be sheer masochism. You have to be willing to try new tastes and look at ways to improve what you are taking, otherwise you may become so bored and negative that you put yourself off the whole plan.

B. Apple, stewed, mixed with a little Udo's Oil (start with one-sixth of a tablespoon) or Missing Link (one-sixth of a table-spoon). If you are very tired, introduce a 'green' food (see page 141).

C. A cup of chicken or vegetable stock (see pages 50–51).

Lunch

Select a meal from the suggestions given in the recipe section for constipation (see pages 51–5).

Sprinkle Udo's Digestive Enzyme on your food. Start by mixing no more than a third of the contents of the capsule with food. Gradually increase the amount until you are able to take the contents of a whole capsule without provoking a reaction. It may take you a month or longer to reach this point, so be patient. If you take too much you may irritate the gut lining.

After you have eaten, dissolve one-quarter of Udo's Super-5 in your mouth. Gradually increase the amount to one tablet after each main meal.

Mid-afternoon

A warm drink of your choice. If you are hungry, choose one of the options given under Mid-morning.

Dinner

Select a meal from the suggestions given in the recipe section for constipation (see pages 51–5). See under Lunch for additional advice.

Bedtime
Dissolve one-quarter of a teaspoon of Cal-M (see page 139) and add to 4–5 cooked stewed prunes.

Diarrhoea Eating Plan

In terms of degeneration, diarrhoea is one step further than constipation. The person whose body copes in this way with the food it is given may not realise it, but there is a high chance that he or she has been constipated for years. The body is merely slipping into the next phase of deterioration. Because so few people can correctly identify constipation, it is usually only when they get diarrhoea that they seek advice. Conventional wisdom is that only when bowel habits change should we consider that something might be wrong and consult a doctor. A woman patient of mine spent years trying to solve the problem of her diarrhoea. She had been to conventional doctors who had investigated it and told her there was nothing clinically wrong with her, and she had tried countless different diets. The last regime she put herself on before coming to me was a low-fat, high-carbohydrate diet. When I saw her for the first time, she was bloated, retaining water and in great pain. Not surprisingly, she felt horrendous.

People who suffer with diarrhoea are especially fragile and their energy levels very low. This woman would often feel as though she was going to pass out. When people are in this state their self-confidence is virtually at zero because they know that whatever they eat is going to cause them pain. This strikes the sufferer at a very basic level. We all know what it is like to 'fail' at something and to bear the disappointment that entails. Any illness strikes at our self esteem, but with the symptoms of diarrhoea it is as though for some reason beyond our understanding we are being denied bodily sustenance. We are not even being denied it by some outside agent, so there is no one to blame but ourselves. It is little wonder that diarrhoea sufferers feel so wretched and so lacking in control over their lives.

Clearly, this state of affairs cannot be changed overnight and the woman in our story had to resign herself to a very strict, boring regime for several weeks before she started to feel better.

Her problem was compounded by the fact of her being a low blood sugar type (see pages 7–8 and 21–3), so I recommended that she have tiny meals every few hours. She knows that it will take months of patience and perseverance to get her digestion right. She is gradually getting her energy back and as she grows stronger she will be able to take more decisions about what she eats. At her present stage she has to be very strict and not deviate from the diet I have worked out for her. She knows that if she eats the wrong food it will blow up in the gut and she will get excruciating pain. Wisely, she does not want to risk this happening and so she is resolutely sticking to my guidelines.

Another diarrhoea patient of mine, after three months on the straight and narrow, discovered what it means to have a body with the energy to cope. One day she decided not to let two rotting bananas on her kitchen table go to waste, so she popped them into her blender and made a shake. She told me later that she had felt slightly strange almost as soon as she had drunk it, but had carried on as normal. That night she felt decidedly unwell, went to the bathroom and was sick. Afterwards she felt fine and went back to bed. I was very pleased when she told me this, because I knew her body had not reacted in this way for a very long time and it signified that her system must be gaining strength as a result of the fermentation changing for the better. The well-functioning digestion has the energy to throw out what it cannot deal with; irritants only remain in the system when the body is too tired to eliminate them. Some of my patients are initially alarmed by their body's new-found vigour and only gradually come to realize that it is a cause for celebration.

Part of the process of getting better is about learning to read your digestive system and understanding its responses to food. The woman in this story knows that if she makes a mistake in future, her body will be strong enough to rectify the problem. She knows, too, that if she had eaten that banana shake with a spoon instead of gulping it down as a drink, and had not compounded this error by having a lunch of starch (which tends to produce the wrong type of fermentation in the gut), her system would probably have coped. Although the journey of discovery is slightly different for each individual, the ground rules are the same for everyone. These have to be learnt and applied if the right type of fermentation is to be promoted and the problem of diarrhoea rectified.

Action Points

Unfortunately for the diarrhoea sufferer, the list of prohibitions is extensive and this automatically limits the scope of the recipes. There is no way round this, I am afraid. Diarrhoea can be likened to a volcano which has to be calmed. You have to think of your digestion as one might a baby's and treat it very gently. I know this is boring, but there is no other way.

As with constipation, only you know how mild or severe your condition is. If it is very bad, you will have to start on very small portions of vegetables steamed in stock. When your system has calmed down, then you will be able to introduce small portions of chicken or fish. There is no hard and fast rule with this. You will have to feel your way slowly. The time it takes to correct the digestion will vary from person to person – one may take a month, while another person may take four or five months. Try not to think of this aspect because it will only put pressure on you. If you can reach the point where you can appreciate the difference between feeling relatively well and feeling lousy, you are on the mend.

Here are your guidelines:

- At the beginning, all food must be cooked, including fruit and vegetables – raw food is out of the question. The aim at this point is to calm the system and not feed the wrong type of fermentation. Only bland, 'baby' foods are appropriate at the start of treatment.

  You must avoid foods that are likely to irritate your gut, such as bran and highly spiced or acidic foods (for example, citrus fruit and beetroot). Foods that leave an acid deposit, such as red meat, are also to be avoided. Oily foods such as avocado are also not appropriate.

  Your digestion does not want to have to work over-time trying to break down highly fibrous vegetables such as brussels sprouts or kale. Carrot, celery, courgette or mange-tout should be less bothersome. It may be that your gut even objects to these, in which case avoid them too and stay on very innocuous dishes, such as the White Herb Risotto or Persian Rice (see pages 56–7), until your digestion is stronger.

- The volume at each meal must not exceed the two-hands principle (see page 5). In some cases even a few spoonfuls too many of stewed apple may ferment badly and cause pain. You must gauge this for yourself.
- Ensure that you sit down to eat – never eat standing up or hurriedly. Chew each mouthful very thoroughly. Try to pre-digest each one before you swallow it; insalivating food well helps to do this. If food is not chewed it cannot be digested and indigestion will result. The right conditions must be created – only you can ensure that they are.
- If you are also a low blood sugar type (see pages 7–8 and 21–3), keep your blood sugar levels balanced by having warm drinks throughout the day as well as ensuring that you take some light sustenance mid-morning and mid-afternoon.
- Neither Acidophilus nor L-glutamine (see pages 138 and 140) should be taken at the start of treatment. Wait until the system has quietened down before introducing them. Both should be taken in tiny amounts initially; take the Acidophilus with meals and sip the L-glutamine, in water, during the day.
- It is important to have warm drinks; cold drinks may shock the digestion into not working and give you stomach cramps. Sip and insalivate them, too; gulping may tense the gut. Generally, green-coloured teas are appropriate for the diarrhoea sufferer. Spicy teas should be avoided.

Plan

On waking
A. Drink two glasses of water (taken from your daily 8 glasses) with a squeeze of natural lemon juice.
B. Cup of camomile tea.

Breakfast
A. Stewed apple and/or pear (see pages 48–9).
B. Stewed fruit with washed and cooked white rice (one-third of total amount – check cupped-hand size to gauge quantity) or powdered slippery elm or Kuzu (see page 68). Either the slippery elm or Kuzu should be mixed with a little water and

then cooked into the stewed fruit. Both agents are calming to the gut lining and take the acid edge off the fruit.

C. Gluten-free breakfast cereal with a little yoghurt or milk. If yoghurt is preferred, ensure that it is a very mild type, otherwise it may encourage acidity.

Mid-morning

Missing Link (see page 141) is too harsh for the gut of the diarrhoea sufferer, so opt instead for a soothing chicken or vegetable stock with appropriate herbs, such as dill (see page 134); if liked, thicken the stock with a little Kuzu. An alternative to stock would be a small portion of bilberry purée.

Lunch

Select a meal from the suggestions given in the recipe section for diarrhoea (see pages 56–9).

A very mild digestive enzyme (Biocare's Digest Aid is excellent – see page 139) can be taken with lunch and dinner. Introduce Acidophilis very gradually once the system has calmed.

Taking charcoal with your meals should help to reduce wind, as should eating some fresh dill, parsley or mint beforehand, and chewing a little aniseed afterwards.

Mid-afternoon

As mid-morning.

Dinner

Select a meal from the suggestions given in the recipe section for diarrhoea (see pages 56–9). See under Lunch for additional advice.

Bedtime

Slippery elm (see page 140)

Irritated Bowel Eating Plan

The person with irritated bowel has reached the stage where the digestive system is so upset it lurches from one extreme to the other: from constipation to diarrhoea and back again. Many sufferers do not understand how they have arrived at this point.

Two stories from my casebook illustrate how irritated bowel can develop out of a way of life.

The first story concerns a man who had suffered for years with poor digestion and whose system was now inflamed. Men can be particularly disadvantaged when it comes to sorting out their health problems, and he was no exception. His job dictated that he keep irregular hours and be constantly on the move. He tended to snatch food while he was on the road, invariably in the company of work-mates whose first port of call when they were hungry would be to visit the nearest 'greasy spoon'. It took him a while after he started coming to me to understand why eschewing a full English breakfast in favour of scrambled eggs on toast would not lessen his digestive problems. As far as his gut was concerned scrambled eggs contain every bit as much protein as the bacon and sausage he had been foregoing; and bread is the worst companion for them. Animal proteins are very acid-forming and if they are eaten without the foil of vegetables, they will further irritate an inflamed digestion.

His dietary situation did not improve when he got home. His wife was not prepared to cook the neutralising, alkali-forming foods which his condition required, and his own culinary skills were non-existent.

My treatments are diet-based so we had to find a way round his particular set of circumstances if he was to continue with me. After a long discussion he went to his mother and asked her if she would help. She agreed and once a week prepares a large vegetable stew which she then divides into portions for him to use from the freezer. He has got into the routine of heating up a portion of the stew and taking it to work with him in a thermos flask.

This regime falls some way short of the ideal, but, given his circumstances, it is the best that can be done. Any compromise in the treatment will obviously have an effect and in his case recovery has been exceedingly slow. However, even limited measures can bring about a marked improvement, and he is starting to feel better, which is the encouragement he needs to persevere.

This man has an ordinary job but one that is by its nature stressful. Many ordinary jobs are like this. They are not high-powered and yet they are very wearing on the body. Sitting in traffic worrying about making an appointment, working irregular hours that make it impossible to establish a rhythm, these are the kinds of stress that nibble away at our health and give us problems with our digestion. In my experience the people who suffer with irritated bowel have spent years over-working their systems in similar ways. Performers are prime examples.

Every time performers go before the public they are putting themselves on the edge, and their body is on the equivalent of 'red alert'. For the body, performing mode is like a war without bloodshed. The damage goes deep, however, and is long-lasting. The worst casualties are those people who have to perform every day. It is little wonder that when they get home they cannot sleep unaided because of the excess of adrenaline surging through them. The whole system – especially the digestion – is put out of kilter by the yo-yo effect which governs their lives. There should be laws protecting people from this systematic abuse. Unfortunately, because it is not recognised as abuse – and performers get a tremendous buzz out of what they do – nothing is done to alert people to the problem. Repetitive gut injury should be as much of an issue as repetitive strain injury.

This syndrome does not only affect well-known actors and actresses, musicians or singers but all performers. The least damaged are those who have the luxury of a few days' grace between performances, enabling them to recover before they put themselves through the experience again. Performers have to look after themselves with extraordinary care and, if they do not, invariably they will run into trouble earlier than people who lead more sedate, less stressful lives. Running on nervous energy automatically blocks the digestion.

As with constipation and diarrhoea, middle age is crunch time for the symptoms of irritated bowel. At this point the gut cuts its supply of enzymes and, as in a game of musical chairs, many people get caught out. An irritated bowel is often the consequence of being caught out and choosing to ignore the fact for many years. Among my patients fitting this category is a woman in her early fifties who had experienced a series of problems with her immune system, principally because she had pushed even harder when her body had sent out signals indicating that it wanted her to do the contrary. A performer, she had relentlessly over-worked her body to the extent where she no longer knew what she was doing. Her gut was in an explosive state, and to the touch was like a fully pumped-up balloon. She had been eating everything raw because she thought it was a healthy thing to do. Raw food is healthy if the digestive system can cope with it. Hers certainly could not and by eating it she had made her situation worse. When I saw her for the first time, she was shaking with tiredness. It is not usually necessary for me to see people every week, but she was in such a state that I felt she needed the contact to help guide her through those difficult first weeks. When there is so little a person can eat without experiencing severe pain, constant encouragement and support are needed to keep them focused on the regime.

We excluded every type of grain, including gluten-free, from her diet. In the beginning the only things she could eat were green cooked vegetables, and small portions of fish or chicken, with vegetable purée mid-morning and mid-afternoon (even stewed apple was too fermenting). She had to put digestive enzymes on every scrap of food. After three weeks of this regime she could cope with eating a crust of bread without blowing up; she could feel it in her stomach, but nothing worse. From this point on she gained in strength and confidence, gradually re-introducing foods she had not been able to eat for years. Because she is a highly strung type, a slight setback would send her into panic mode, fearful she would be plunged back to where she was before she came to me. When she did something wrong, she would become groggy and feel slightly hungover – a sensation she called a 'food hangover'. As her body became more alkaline and the fermentation improved, these upsets did not recur and after five months she was able to cope with most foods well.

Action Points

Do not give up before you start. The regime for irritated bowel is necessarily strict and very limited. Great determination is required to see it through to the end, especially as that end is not a fixed point. How quickly your gut heals will depend on you. Here are your guidelines:

- Eat little and often. How little will depend on the state of your gut. The aim is to get your body to digest what you are giving it and simultaneously to repair and restore the 'friendly' bacterial flora. You can assist this process by chewing very thoroughly and taking the mildest model of digestive enzyme with meals (instructions are given below). How much of the capsule you can take will depend on the state of your particular gut. Start with a tiny amount; try one-quarter of a capsule and monitor your body's reaction: Are you getting windy? Are your stools slightly looser or firmer?
- Most IBS sufferers are also low blood sugar types (see pages 7–8 and 21–3), which goes some way towards explaining the state of their gut and why they have not been digesting their food. It is important that you keep your energy levels up by having warm drinks throughout the day as well as ensuring that you take some light sustenance mid-morning and mid-afternoon.
- Expect setbacks. If you make a wrong decision and your gut objects, resign yourself to four or five days of getting back on track. Your ability to recover will improve as the body gains in strength.
- Be patient. The length of time you have had IBS, your general health and constitution are among the factors that will determine how long it takes you to get over it. I have had patients who could barely eat anything without suffering – even a food as innocuous as vegetable stock could not be tolerated. For people in this state it may take months to get them to the stage where the gut does not react. Your attitude, emotional state and how closely you stick to the plan are the most powerful weapons at your disposal to ensure a successful outcome. Use them.

Plan

The initial phase of IBS treatment involves quietening the gut so that it does not explode every time you eat. In this respect it is very similar to that for diarrhoea in the early stages. However, because IBS involves two extremes – diarrhoea and constipation – the plan depends on you using it flexibly to cover both tendencies.

I have included eating suggestions which cover both eventualities. It is up to you to use them appropriately.

At some point after you have gently started to correct the fermentation, your body will stop oscillating between these two extremes and settle into one of them, usually constipation. Take this as a sign that your gut is getting better. It is imperative, however, that you proceed at a snail's pace with the supplements I suggest you take. Only tiny amounts will be tolerated in the beginning, by which I mean fractions of the recommended dose. If too much is introduced too quickly you may find yourself becoming more constipated rather than less, or experiencing a bout of diarrhoea.

If at any point you swing into the extremes of IBS, go back to either the constipation or diarrhoea plan (see pages 32–7 for constipation and pages 37–41 for diarrhoea) for guidance as to how you should proceed.

On waking
A. Drink two glasses of water (taken from your daily 8 glasses) with a few drops of natural lemon juice; if you are tending towards diarrhoea, begin very slowly with one drop of lemon and gauge your system's response. If even this amount proves too strong for your system, opt for chamomile tea instead.

Breakfast
A. Stewed apple or pear; suitable for both phases, (see pages 48–9).
B. Oat or oatbran porridge (see page 49) with some grated apple or a few slices of papaya; suitable for constipation phase.
C. Gluten-free cereal with stewed fruit; may be suitable for both phases.

Mid-morning
A. Take about one-quarter of a teaspoon of Udo's Oil (to heal the gut lining) mixed with some stewed apple or pear. If you are very windy, use puréed vegetable instead of the fruit or one of the stocks (see pages 49–51). Add a little 'green energy' food (see page 141) if you are feeling tired. *Note:* Missing Link is not an appropriate energy-booster for those in the diarrhoea phase.
B. Lemon and olive oil drink (see page 48); use only when in constipation phase.

Lunch

Select a meal appropriate to the phase you are in from the suggestions given in the recipe section for IBS (see pages 59–63).

Get into the habit of chewing a few fresh herbs before you eat a meal. Whatever is in season will be appropriate – mint, tarragon or basil, for example. The herbs will alert your digestion to the fact that food is on its way and it had better prepare to receive it.

In the diarrhoea phase, take one capsule of Biocare's Digest Aid with your meal. Later, when your condition is improving and you have settled into constipation, I would recommend that you introduce a stronger digestive enzyme, such as Udo's Ultimate Digestive Enzyme Blend.

After your meal, help the digestion further by sipping a teaspoon of rosewater in warm water. If you do not like the taste of rosewater, try chamomile instead. I would also advise that you introduce Acidophilus very slowly, starting with about one-tenth of a tablet of Udo's Super-5 after meals. Over the course of about a month this amount should be gradually increased to one whole tablet. Much later (perhaps after two months) I would suggest that you move on to a stronger model, such as Gut Reaction Probion.

Mid-afternoon

A. Stewed fruit mixed with Udo's Oil; see note above re Udo's Oil in diarrhoea phase.

B. Lemon and olive oil drink (see page 48); specifically for constipation tendency.

Dinner

Select appropriately from the recipes given on pages 59–63. Also see under Lunch for additional advice.

Bedtime

In diarrhoea phase, take slippery elm (see page 140). In constipation phase, have a fibre drink, such as Transitibiane (see Fibre, page 140), or a few stewed prunes.

Chapter Five

RECIPES FOR THE EATING PLANS

BASICS

Lemon and Olive Oil Drink/Sauce

These two ingredients are probably the constipated person's most helpful friends. Together they give the liver the lift it needs. Some people find this drink a bit hard to take. If you do, try using the mixture as a sauce for protein and vegetable dishes. If the option is open to you, use an organic lemon because this recipe requires the whole fruit, including the rind and pips.

  1 medium lemon
  1 tbsp of cold-pressed virgin olive oil
  300–450 ml ($^{1}/_{2}$–$^{3}/_{4}$ pt) lemon or apple juice, or water

Quarter the lemon and place in a blender. Add the juice or water, then the olive oil. Process at high speed for about two minutes. Strain, discarding the pulp.

Stewed Apple or Pear

This can be prepared in advance and kept in the fridge for you to use as required. If you do not have time to do this, buy sugar-free ready-prepared fruit purée from your health shop. Use only green eating apples; red varieties do not contain the pectin found in green apples.

Wash the unpeeled apples or pears, then slice them and place in a saucepan with a little water. Cook them until they are soft.

Alternatively, bake them in the oven and at the end of cooking grate some fresh ginger and sprinkle this with a little cinnamon over them.

Oatbran Porridge

Grate a washed, unpeeled green apple and set aside. Mix oatbran with water in a small saucepan. Cook the mixture until it is the right consistency for you. Mix in the apple. Remove from the heat. Serve in a bowl topped with a little yoghurt.

Stocks

When the digestion is badly out of kilter, stocks are a gentle means of getting nutrients into the body without causing offence. The only problem with them is that they are time-consuming to prepare. I have provided a few tips on preparation for those who have the time and the inclination to do their own from scratch. For those of you who are groaning at the thought, I would advise you to look around, make enquiries and see if you can find a good source of ready-made stocks. There are people out there who make perfect examples, as I have found to my great joy. If you try and fail, write to me and I shall reveal my source.

Ingredients
For meat stocks, ensure the bones smell fresh. Trim off any obvious fat. Roasting them beforehand removes a lot of the fat and is said to add flavour to the final stock.

Onions, carrots and celery are the basis of a good vegetable stock. Do not use vegetables that are liable to impart a bitter taste: cabbage, lettuce, aubergine, and celery leaves tend to do this.

Cooking
As soon as the liquid reaches boiling point, reduce the heat so that it bubbles along at a gentle simmer. Skim off any foam as it forms. Do not cover the cooking pot.

Cooling
After cooking, transfer the stock to a glass or ceramic container to

help it cool; plastic tends to retain heat. Place in a refrigerator if the stock is required in a hurry or place the container in a bowl of iced water.

When the stock is cool, remove the fat on top, cover the container and place in the refrigerator, where it will keep for up to ten days. Alternatively, divide the stock into smaller containers and freeze.

Vegetable Stock

Makes approx. 3 litres (5^1/$_4$ pt)

1 large leek, trimmed, rinsed and chopped
2 medium onions, peeled and chopped
3 carrots, peeled and chopped
2 sticks of celery, trimmed and chopped
1 small bunch flat-leaved parsley, rinsed and chopped
3 bay leaves
2 tsp dried marjoram
^{1}/$_2$ tsp dried thyme

Place all the vegetables and herbs in a large saucepan and pour over 4 litres (7 pt) water. Bring to the boil, reduce to a simmer and cook gently, uncovered, for about 1 hour.

Strain through a fine sieve, then allow to cool. Refrigerate or freeze until required.

This choice of vegetables is mine, of course. You can adapt the recipe as you like. Try to use fresh herbs, the parsley stems will impart the flavour of the herb without the bitterness that sometimes comes with cooking parsley leaves.

Chicken Stock

Makes approx. 2.4 litres (4 pt)

1.3 kg (3 lb) organic chicken, jointed and cleaned
2 carrots, peeled and chopped
2 sticks celery, trimmed and chopped

1 large onion, peeled and chopped
4 garlic cloves, peeled and halved
1 bay leaf
12 whole peppercorns

Preheat the oven to 190°C/375°F/Gas Mark 5. Wash and pat dry the chicken pieces and place in a shallow roasting tin. Bake in the oven for 35–40 minutes until golden and tender. Drain on absorbent kitchen paper.

Transfer the chicken to a large saucepan and pour over 3.6 litres (6 pt) cold water. Gradually bring to the boil, and skim away the scum that forms on the top of the saucepan using a slotted flat spoon.

Add the remaining ingredients, reduce the heat, cover and simmer gently, undisturbed for 3 hours.

Strain the stock and allow to cool. Chill uncovered until the fat hardens, then remove. Refrigerate or freeze until required.

MAIN MEALS: CONSTIPATION

Avocado or Smoked Salmon with Pear

Serves 2

This recipe is very versatile and serves very nicely as a lunch or light supper dish, or even as a starter.

1 large ripe avocado or 150 g (6 oz) smoked salmon
1 ripe pear, washed and sliced
Rocket
Fresh herbs; rosemary, fennel seeds and fresh, grated ginger go
    particularly well with this combination

If using the avocado, peel it and place the two halves on separate plates. Alternatively, arrange the smoked salmon on the plates. Slice the pear and put it with the rocket in a separate bowl. Hand out the sauce and the fresh herbs separately.

Grilled Fish with Lemon Grass

Serves 2

2 pieces of white, firm fish, each weighing about 125 g (5 oz)

Marinade
1 tbsp olive oil
1 clove garlic, crushed
1/2 stalk lemon grass, trimmed and finely chopped
1/2 tsp sesame oil
1 tbsp Braggs Aminos
Juice of 1 lime
1/2 tsp curry powder
1/2 tsp five-spice powder
1/2 tsp honey

Garnish
Fresh coriander

Mix the ingredients for the marinade. Place the fish in it, ensuring that every piece is well coated. Leave for 1 hour; turn the pieces at least once during this period.

Remove the fish. Grill each side for 3–4 minutes or until just cooked. Remove to warm plates and baste each piece of fish with remaining marinade. Sprinkle with coriander leaves and serve with french beans and braised celery.

Mint, Lime and Cumin Lamb with Roast Fennel

Serves 4

900 g (2 lb) lamb for roasting
Juice of 2 limes
15 g (1/2 oz) fresh mint, finely chopped
Crushed cumin
2 large (or 4 medium) fennel bulbs
2 tbsp cold-pressed virgin olive oil
Salt and freshly ground black pepper

Rub into the lamb the juice of the lime, the chopped mint and the crushed cumin. Roast in an oven pre-heated to 180°C/350°F/Gas Mark 4 for 1 to 1¹/4 hours, depending on how pink you like it.

Meanwhile, prepare the fennel, trimming the top and removing any coarse outer layers. Cut into quarters, rinse with cold water and dry thoroughly.

Place in a small roasting tray and turn in the olive oil. Season with salt and black pepper.

Roast at 230°C/450°F/Gas Mark 8 for about 25 minutes or until the vegetables are tender. Baste at least once during cooking.

Serve with a little lemon and olive oil sauce (see page 48) and steamed broccoli or french beans.

Mild Spiced Chicken with Spinach

Serves 2

¹/2 tbsp olive oil
15 g (¹/2 oz) butter
¹/2 onion, chopped
¹/2 clove garlic, crushed
1 x 2.5 cm/1 in piece root ginger, finely chopped
¹/4 fresh chilli, deseeded and finely chopped
2 chicken breasts, cut into cubes
1 courgette, chopped
1 stick celery, finely chopped
150 ml (5 fl oz) chicken stock (see page 50)
265 ml (7 fl oz) yoghurt
Salt and pepper
265 g (7 oz) prepared baby spinach leaves

Heat the oil and butter in a frying pan and gently fry the onion for 10 minutes. Add the garlic, ginger, chilli and curry powder and fry for 5 minutes. Add the chicken breasts and cook until browned all over. Add the stock, celery and courgette. Simmer rapidly until the stock is almost absorbed, then reduce the heat and add the yoghurt. Season. Add the spinach and cook for another 2–3 minutes, until the spinach begins to wilt.

Serve with fresh coriander leaves, lime wedges and vegetables of your choice.

Persian Stew

Serves 4

900 g (2 lb) lamb cut into 5cm (2in) cubes
2 onions, finely chopped
150 g (5 oz) fresh fenugreek, chopped, or 1 tbsp dried
    fenugreek
6 dried limes
450 g (16 oz) broad beans
300 g (10 oz) fresh chives, chopped
300 g (10 oz) continental parsley, chopped
150 g (5 oz) lemon juice
1 bunch coriander, chopped
3 tbsp olive oil
Salt and pepper

Sauté the seasoned meat and onions in 1 tbsp of olive oil until golden brown. Add boiling water to cover and let the ingredients simmer until the meat is almost cooked.

In a separate pan, fry the vegetables in the rest of the olive oil. Add to the meat. Pierce the skin of the washed limes with a meat skewer before adding them to the meat in the pan. Allow this mixture to simmer on a low heat for another half-hour until the limes and meat are cooked. Adjust the flavour with lemon juice to taste. Add the beans and simmer for a few minutes more.

Serve with selected vegetables.

Spicy Green Lentil Stew

Serves 6

The ingredients for this may seem daunting but all of them should be available in your supermarket.

It is important to neutralise the wind-forming tendency of the lentils by pre-soaking them. Allow a couple of days for this: one day for soaking, changing the water every few hours, and the second day for leaving the lentils to lie, as though you were sprouting them.

4 tbsp olive oil
1 large onion, chopped
Salt to taste
2 tsp turmeric
6 cloves garlic, 3 of them crushed, the remainder finely
    chopped
350 g (12 oz) green lentils
1 tbsp curry powder
1 stalk lemon grass, bruised
3 pieces star anise.
1 cinnamon stick
2 large carrots, roughly chopped
Juice of 1 lime
2 red chillies, deseeded and chopped
Chopped mint leaves
$1/8$ tsp asafoetida/hing (see Store Cupboard, page 65)

Mix the lentils, onion, turmeric and crushed garlic with 3 tablespoons of the olive oil. Marinate for at least 1 hour, or up to 24 hours in the fridge.

To cook, place the remaining oil in a saucepan and fry the chopped garlic until slightly golden. Add the curry powder, lemon grass, star anise and cinnamon stick, then the lentils and other marinaded ingredients. Add water – enough to almost but not quite cover the ingredients. Bring to the boil, then reduce heat to a gentle simmer. Cook for almost an hour. Add the carrots and simmer until they are just cooked (about 5 10 minutes). Stir in the lime juice.

Serve with rice, sprinkled with fresh mint and red chillies.

MAIN MEALS: DIARRHOEA

White Herb Risotto

Serves 4

> 3 tbsp olive oil
> 2 sticks celery
> 250 g (9 oz) white arborio rice
> 700 ml (25 fl oz) vegetable stock (see page 50)
> 3 tbsp chopped fresh dill
> Salt and freshly ground black pepper
> 1 tbsp extra virgin olive oil

Heat the oil in a heavy-bottomed pan. Add the celery and cook gently for 5–10 minutes. Add the rice, stirring well. Add the stock (which should be hot) gradually, allowing a ladleful at a time and waiting until this has been absorbed before adding more. After about 15 minutes, stir in the dill. Continue cooking until all the stock has been used up and the rice is tender (about half an hour). Season and before serving, stir in the tablespoon of extra virgin oil.

Serve with cooked courgettes and celery.

Persian Rice

Serves 4

> 250 g (9 oz) white basmati rice
> 1 tsp salt
> 3 tbsp olive oil

Soak the rice for 2 hours in water, then drain and rinse.

Bring a large saucepan of water to the boil, add the salt and rice and boil uncovered for 3–4 minutes until the grains of rice are slightly tender but still opaque.

Drain and rinse the rice in cold running water to remove the excess starch. Shake off the excess water and place back in the saucepan. Make indents into the rice using the end of a wooden spoon and drizzle in the olive oil.

Stand the saucepan over a very low heat, cover the pan with a clean tea towel and then a tight-fitting lid. Cook undisturbed for 30 minutes until the rice is tender and fluffy, and the grains on the bottom of the saucepan are crisp. Fork through and serve.

Variation
You can layer the rice in the saucepan with chopped herbs of your choice.

Chicken with Herb Broth

Serves 4

2 large leeks, trimmed and cut in half lengthways
8 small carrots, peeled
1 x 1.5 kg (3 lb) chicken
500 ml (18 fl oz) chicken stock (see page 50)
200 g (7 oz) runner beans, sliced and blanched for 2 minutes
2 tbsp grated fresh horseradish
1 large bunch fresh chervil
Salt and freshly ground black pepper

Put the leeks and carrots in a pot that is just large enough to take all the ingredients, including the chicken. Sit the chicken on top of the bed of vegetables and pour in the stock; if the chicken is not covered, add some water to the pot. Bring to the boil, cover and cook just below simmering point for about 45 minutes. Skim frequently so that at the end of the cooking time the broth is very clear. Add the runner beans, horseradish and chervil to the broth and cook for a few minutes longer. Season to taste.

Herb Omelette with Light Herb Sauce

Serves 2

Sauce
300 ml (10 fl oz) chicken or vegetable stock (see page 50)
15 g (1/2 oz) finely chopped fresh green herbs (such as parsley, dill, thyme and tarragon)

Omelette
4 eggs
25 g (1 oz) butter
15 g (1/2 oz) finely chopped fresh green herbs (as above)

Put the stock and three-quarters of the herbs in a saucepan and simmer, covered, for 30 minutes over a very low heat. Strain the resulting liquid through a sieve into a clean pan, squeezing as much of the juice from the herbs as possible. Discard the pulp. Reduce the sauce to about one-third by boiling hard and then season it with salt and pepper. Put aside.

Whisk the eggs in a bowl with 1 tbsp of water, season well, then mix in the herbs. Heat half the butter in an omelette pan. At this point return the juice to the heat so that it can warm through while the omelette is cooking. Pour half the egg mixture into the pan just before the butter turns brown. Cook quickly, lifting up the edges of the omelette as it sets to allow the uncooked mixture to reach the heat. Do not over-cook. Remove from the pan when the centre is still runny, folding one side over onto the other. Slide onto a warm plate, surround with some of the re-heated herb sauce, and serve. No omelette worth the name should ever be left to languish while others are cooked in its wake!

Cook the second omelette – as it will be yours, it will not matter if you are the one kept waiting.

Spring Chicken with Mange-tout and Fennel

Serves 2

2 small spring chickens or poussins (or use chicken pieces)
4 tbsp olive oil
Juice of 1 lemon
$1/2$ tsp paprika
$3/4$ tsp coarse sea salt
$1/2$ tsp ground cumin
Pinch cayenne pepper
2 tbsp finely chopped continental parsley
Mange-tout
Fennel
Toasted cumin seeds

Mix together the oil, herbs, salt and spices and turn the poussins or chicken pieces in it so they are thoroughly coated. Remove the chicken to a separate dish and put in the fridge to marinate for at least 2 hours. Reserve the remainder of the marinade.

Heat the grill and cook the chicken under it for at least 30 minutes, regularly basting with the marinade and turning the birds or pieces.

When the poussins or chicken pieces are cooked, remove them to warm plates and serve with fresh lemon wedges, and cooked mange-tout and fennel sprinkled with toasted cumin seeds.

MAIN MEALS: IBS

Grilled Fish with Dill and Lemon and Olive Oil Sauce

Serves 2

Adjusted slightly, this meal would be appropriate for both phases of IBS. If you are in the diarrhoea phase, use the sauce sparingly if at all.

    2 fillets or pieces of salmon or firm white fish
    1 tbsp lemon juice
    1 tbsp continental parsley, chopped
    150 ml (5 fl oz) lemon and olive oil sauce (see page 48)
    1 tbsp dill, chopped
    1 tbsp onion, chopped
    1 tbsp capers, rinsed
    Salt

Marinate the fish with lemon juice and a pinch of salt. Refrigerate. Combine the rest of the ingredients, cover and refrigerate for 1–2 hours.

Pre-heat the grill. Spread half the ingredients mixture over one side of the fish pieces. Grill one side, then turn and spread the remaining mixture over the other sides of the fish. Grill until the fish flakes easily.

Serve with steamed courgettes. Hand round the sauce separately.

Lemon Chicken

Serves 4

This recipe includes several ingredients which, if used in too large quantities, may upset the very sensitive stomach. If your stomach is in this category, drastically reduce the quantities of paprika, cayenne and onion and use them only in tiny amounts.

1.5 kg (3^1/2 lb) chicken
2 slices of lemon
150 ml (5 fl oz) fresh lemon juice
2 tbsp chicken stock (see page 50)
2 tbsp olive oil
1 large onion, sliced thinly
2 cloves garlic, crushed
1 tbsp paprika
Pinch of cayenne pepper
Salt and ground black pepper

Season the chicken with the salt and pepper inside and out. Put lemon slices inside the bird and place in an ovenproof dish. Use the onion, garlic and stock as a marinade, scattering and pouring them over the chicken. Refrigerate for 2 hours.

Pre-heat the oven to 180°C/450°F/Gas Mark 4. Remove the chicken from fridge. Sprinkle the paprika and cayenne pepper over the bird. Place in the oven and cook for about 1^1/2 hours, basting occasionally and turning the chicken over in the juices.

Serve with cooked vegetables of your choice.

Smoked Trout with Spinach and Pear

Serves 2

Grilled fresh trout is also good with this combination of fruit and vegetable. Those of you who are in the diarrhoea phase may need to be sparing with the spinach and the lemon and olive oil sauce.

2 trout, organic, smoked
1 pear, washed and sliced
Spinach

Lemon and oil sauce (see page 48)
Fresh dill

Put the spinach in a saucepan to sweat over a gentle heat while you arrange the slices of pear on the plates with the fish. Sprinkle with fresh dill. When the spinach is done, serve with lemon wedges and a few spoonfuls of lemon and olive oil sauce.

Aubergine or Courgette Rice

Serves 6

Which vegetable you choose will depend on your preference and the state of your gut. Some people find aubergines difficult to take. Much of the bitterness can be eliminated by sprinkling the sliced aubergines with salt before they are fried. Courgettes, too, benefit from this treatment.

The type of rice you should choose will depend on which phase you are in: use white basmati if you are tending towards diarrhoea, and brown wholegrain if you are tending towards constipation.

275 g (10 oz) rice
3 small aubergines or 6 courgettes
2 tbsp barberries (see page 132)
1 tsp powdered saffron dissolved in 1 tbsp hot water and 1 tsp honey
1 tbsp honey for the barberries
2 eggs
100 g (4 oz) plain yoghurt (goat or sheep's)
Olive oil
Butter
Salt

Soak the rice in water and a little salt for 2 hours before cooking.

Slice the aubergines or courgettes and salt them. Let them stand for half an hour in a colander. Pat dry with paper kitchen towel. Fry in a little olive oil. Remove from the pan and place on a kitchen towel to soak up the oil.

Cut the tails of the barberries and wash quickly. Do not soak. Dry with a kitchen towel. Fry with a little olive oil and add the tablespoon of honey. Put to one side.

Drain the rice. Bring a large saucepan of water to the boil, add the salt and drained rice and boil uncovered for 3–4 minutes until the rice is cooked.

Beat the eggs and mix with the yoghurt, saffron, 1 tablespoon of olive oil and half the cooked rice.

Place the rice mixture in an ovenproof dish. Put sliced pieces of butter on top and around the rice. Flatten top with back of spoon. Layer the mixture with the fried aubergines or courgettes. Add the rest of the rice and flatten top again.

Cover the dish and place in an oven at 180°C/350°F/Gas Mark 4 for about 45–50 minutes or until the mixture has the appearance of a cake.

Remove the dish from the oven and turn contents out onto a hot serving dish. Sprinkle the fried barberries on top. Serve hot with additional cooked vegetables of your choice.

Pea and Mint Soup

Serves 4

This can be made into a complete meal by serving it before slices of avocado sprinkled with fresh herbs and a little lemon and olive oil sauce (see page 48). Those in the diarrhoea phase may like to try just some of the soup.

    1 tsp olive oil
    2 tbsp onion, chopped
    1 tsp garlic, finely chopped
    2 tbsp leek, chopped
    450 g (1 lb) peas, frozen
    600 ml (20 fl oz) vegetable stock (see page 50)
    1/4 tsp salt
    1/2 tsp ground black pepper
    4 mint leaves, finely sliced
    3 tbsp plain yoghurt (goat, sheep or soya)

Heat the olive oil in a saucepan. Sauté the onion, garlic and leek over a medium heat until the onions are translucent.

Add the peas and vegetable stock and cook for a further 8–10 minutes.

Pour the soup into a blender and blend until smooth. Season with salt and pepper. Return to the saucepan.

In a separate small dish, combine the mint and yoghurt, mixing well.

Ladle the hot soup into individual bowls and garnish with 1 tablespoon of the yoghurt and mint mixture.

Vegetable Stir-Fry

Serves 6

3 tbsp olive oil
2 onions, thinly sliced
2 cloves garlic, crushed
1 tsp fresh root ginger, shredded
Salt

Sauce
2 tbsp Braggs Liquid Aminos (see page 65)
2 tbsp stock or water
$1/2$ tsp honey

Vegetables
110 g (4 oz) carrots, sliced finely
110 g (4 oz) baby corns
110 g (4 oz) mange-tout
110 g (4 oz) broccoli florets
1 red pepper, cored, deseeded and sliced finely
110 g (4 oz) cauliflower, sliced
50 g (2 oz) Chinese leaves or cabbage, roughly chopped
1 stalk celery, finely chopped

Heat the oil in a wok or large frying pan. Over a moderate heat for about 1 minute cook the onions, garlic, ginger and salt. Add the vegetables and cook until they are tender.

Mix the stock, honey and Braggs Aminos into a smooth paste and stir into the vegetables in the wok or pan. Serve.

Chapter Six

FEEDING IDEAS

One of the hardest parts of changing how we eat is overcoming the terror of parting from old and exceedingly tasty 'friends'. The question 'What on earth am I going to eat?' will loom very large. I was forced to confront this question when I made the decision to try to help my own digestive problems by changing my diet. I am the worst case I have ever treated, so I know how difficult it can be. Eating proper starch makes me fall asleep and even gluten-free pasta or flour is problematic for my digestion. I was determined, though, not to become a diet martyr – one of those people who will stoically eat the inedible just because they have been told it is good for them. I have to like what is good for me, otherwise I will leave it alone and find something else. I want to be a happy healthy person. Misery and good health are mutually exclusive, and no diet – however wonderful the components – will work if you feel resentful.

The decision to cook in a way that suits our own digestion ought to be viewed as an exciting opportunity, a turning away from the mundane and predictable. For people who like food enough to make it taste interesting, this decision should be liberating and mark the beginning of an enjoyable journey. I have spent years on this journey and still find it exciting. The range of foods I eat is continually expanding as new products become available. Ten years ago there was only a fraction of the variety we have now. Thankfully, we are living through a golden age of food and the opportunities for increasing one's options seem limitless.

The foods listed below reflect my likes and dislikes. The aim is not for you to try to like everything I recommend. Try each item by all means, but do not feel obliged to like them. These are the basic foodstuffs which I ensure I have in stock at all times. It is important that you should build your own store cupboard because all your good intentions will go for nothing if you continue to stock ingredients which do not support your particular dietary requirements. I know that if I have not had time to pre-plan a meal I can improvise with what I have in my cupboards to produce a healthy (for me), delicious dish.

When the gut is in better shape, you should not hesitate to broaden your diet. Use the glossaries of foods and herbs (pages 102–44) to learn about the qualities of a wide range of ingredients. Experienced cooks will no doubt relish the idea of devising new dishes using these. However, following this brief section you will find a selection of maintenance meals which you may wish to use or adapt to suit your taste (see pages 72–93).

Gudrun's Store Cupboard

Asafoetida/hing

Use to make lentils or any pulses less wind forming and more easily digestable. I always add a pinch ($1/8$th tsp) when I cook pulses. It is available from any Indian supermarket.

Biosalt

This is my chosen salt because it has added potassium, one of the minerals which tends to be drawn out of the body by ordinary salt. I like the taste too.

Braggs Liquid Aminos

This looks and tastes like soy sauce while containing less salt and offering all the amino acids required by the body. I use it instead of a soy sauce and will squirt it onto rice, vegetables or whatever food I want to give extra bite to. Braggs is also alkalising.

Cider vinegar

A couple of tablespoons of cider vinegar in warm water, sweetened with honey, is a wonderfully cheap means of making the body more alkaline – if you can bear the taste. I cannot and will instead use Cal-M (see page 139) or lemon and ginger. I do like cider vinegar as a condiment, however, and use it in preference to other types of vinegar, which tend to be acid-forming. I grow a variety of herbs on my allotment and when these are ready I make my own range of herb-flavoured vinegars, with cider vinegar as the basis. I may, for example, chop up some garlic and basil or ginger and chives, or thyme, whatever takes my fancy, so that I have a variety of flavours at my disposal for dressing salads. When I want to soften the tart edge of the vinegar, I add a little honey (always Manuka honey, which tastes good and aids the lining of the stomach).

Coconut milk

I use this quite often simply because I like the taste. I use it for sauces or to 'lift' stir-fried vegetables, perhaps with the addition of some lemon grass and ginger, which I think go very well with it. Coconut is quite a fatty food, but only a little is required to make a difference to a dish so do not let this put you off trying it.

Coffee

This makes the body very acid. There are a few benign alternatives, such as barley cup and chicory, but they are not to everyone's taste. I ask my patients to restrict their coffee intake as much as they can bear without becoming completely miserable. If this means they enjoy all the more the one cup a day they allow themselves, that is fine.

Dairy products

I avoid cow's protein and will opt for either goat's or sheep's products instead, preferably goat's. If I cannot get sheep's milk, I will use ordinary cow's milk. When it comes to cheese, I prefer the taste of sheep's cheese to goat's cheese, which is too bland for my palate. Two favourite cheeses are Priscilla, a soft sheep cheese, and Troy, a delicious organic hard cheese; both are in the Stamp Collection range of foods.

I use very little butter because I cannot eat bread, which makes my blood sugar levels swing wildly, but when I do, I always use organic from cows. Sometimes I will bend my own rules and put a little of it on my vegetables after cooking. Delicious!

Eggs *(organic)*

I use only the yolk of the egg because my digestion cannot cope with the white part. If I want a quick meal I will stir-fry some vegetables in stock and near the end of cooking drop an egg yolk on top. This finishing touch always brings back exciting memories of my first visit to Florence.

Fruit

I always have a selection of seasonal fruit. My favourites are apples, avocados, lemons, limes, pears and papaya. I also like to keep a few jars of stewed fruit in the cupboard which I use for mixing with Udo's Oil or Missing Link.

Ginger

I use root ginger a lot in cooking and as an ingredient in alkalising drinks. Every morning in my bath I sip a mug of lemon juice in boiling water spiked with a slice of ginger and, if my spirits need raising, a teaspoon of honey.

I adore the tartness of pickled ginger too. This is often called Sushi Ginger and is used on fish, rice and tempura. Sometimes I put some in a salad but mostly I chop it up and have it as a side dish.

Herbs

My favourites are saffron, root ginger, garlic and lemon grass. I am also very partial to fenugreek, dill, mint, thyme, sage and basil, all of which I grow on my allotment. If fresh herbs are difficult to come by in the winter months, I make do with them in dried form.

Herb teas

These are a pleasant way of keeping up one's liquid intake. Although I impress on others the virtues of bottled mineral water, I find it very difficult to drink myself, especially during the colder months of the year. The fact that I am a low blood sugar type is mostly responsible for this – I need warmth. There is a huge range of herb teas available from supermarkets and healthfood shops. I tend not to use these, preferring my own concoctions. Lemon and ginger tea is undoubtedly my favourite, but I also like to infuse fresh rosemary, lemon grass and fennel. After a meal I often make a digestive drink by adding 1–2 teaspoons of rosewater to a little warm water.

Honey

Despite being a low blood sugar type, I always have a jar of Manuka honey in my cupboard. This delicious thick, raw honey comes from New Zealand and is valued for its healing properties, especially against *Helicobacter pylori*, the bacterium believed to be at the root of the majority of cases of ulcerated or inflamed stomach ulcers.

Juices

I often have a carton of organic juice in the fridge. Beetroot is a regular because it is such a friend to the liver. For taste, though, I love the exoticism of juices made from fruits like guava.

Kuzu *(Clearspring)*

This is a special arrowroot for very sensitive systems which are liable to be upset by the standard thickening agents. It is highly absorbable and appropriate for anyone – including children – in whom the digestion is out of sorts, especially with diarrhoea.

Lemon grass

Together with coconut this is the 'taste' of Thai cuisine. I like its warming aspect and use it in a variety of vegetable dishes.

Lime Leaves

I invariably add a few chopped lime leaves to vegetable stews to give the food the tart flavour I like.

Missing Link

Because I am a low blood sugar type, I need to feed my body between meals and this product, which is composed of a wide range of plant-based 'super-foods', can be mixed with juice, yoghurt or stewed fruit to make a nourishing snack. (See also page 118).

Natural Mineral Water

Try various brands as each displays its typical mineral analysis on the label and you will be able to select the brand or brands that best suit your taste and your particular health need. Refrigerate once open. (See also pages 128–9.)

Oatbran

This forms the basis of my breakfast in the winter months – see page 49 for recipe. I find it delightfully warming and its low glycaemic response is especially good for a low blood sugar type such as myself.

Oils

The two oils I stock are olive oil and Udo's Ultimate Oil Blend. Occasionally I cook with olive oil but more often I use it, mixed with lemon, as a condiment for salads and proteins. I always have some of this mixture already prepared so I can use it immediately. As with cider vinegar, I make my own flavoured oils from the herbs I grow. Sometimes I make a thickened version of the lemon and olive oil drink (see page 48), incorporating different herbs, and use it as one might a Hollandaise sauce.

Udo's Oil is a necessary luxury for me. Most of us do not have enough oils and those we do ingest are often rancid. I use Udo's to keep my blood sugar levels even. It is expensive compared with other oils, but I know that it has been processed correctly to take account of its volatile essential fatty acids. Udo's is a tasty way of ensuring that I get these in the correct proportions.

Pasta

I cannot eat wheat products of any kind, and even gluten-free pasta or buckwheat or rice noodles are not options for me. My 'pasta' is a very nutritious and exciting, black, pre-cooked type of seaweed. I cook it as one would pasta, mixed with whichever vegetables are in season and take my fancy.

Pepper (black, white and cayenne)

I have no special dietary reason for stocking these spices – I just like them on or with certain foods. I like especially the warming effect of cayenne.

Pesto

I use this as a spiky addition to cooked vegetables. You might like to try it on crackers or with buckwheat or rice noodles.

Rice

I can cope with the starch in rice if I cook the grains the way the Iranians do, by cooking it until it is almost ready, rinsing it and then cooking it to completion with herbs – see page 56. My favourite types of rice are brown basmati and jasmine rice (also called flavoured Thai rice). Both absorb water without becoming too sticky and starchy.

Saffron

I love the colour and taste of saffron and use it a lot in cooking. In Indian cuisine it is used particularly for celebratory occasions, partly reflecting its high cost relative to other spices but also its character – certainly, it makes me feel happy whenever I eat it. I buy Iranian saffron, which is significantly cheaper than Indian saffron and just as good. My favourite sauce incorporating saffron also includes chopped root ginger and fine slivers of lemon rind and uses goat yoghurt as its base – it is delicious and can transform any boring dish.

Seaweed Tartare *(Bord à Bord)*

As its name suggests, this is a tartare sauce made of seaweed. The taste of seaweed is generally too strong for most people's palates. This sauce should convert a few doubters – it certainly did me. I like it on avocado but it can just as easily be spread onto biscuits or bread or used as a dip. However you eat it, the taste is delicious.

Stock

Fresh stock is better than stock cubes and I always have some in the fridge, often bought from an organic source and then frozen into squares. Invariably, the chicken stock I use is in this form because I am too lazy to make my own. Vegetable stock is comparatively easy to do – we waste so much in the leaves and tops we trim from our vegetables. When combined with a few herbs of one's choice these can make very good – and cheap – stock. See stock recipes on pages 49–51.

Sweeteners

I avoid using cane sugar and instead opt for fructose, maple syrup and Oligo-fibre. See the entry for Sugar in A–Z of Foods, page 126.

Tahini

Creamed sesame makes a nice spread for bread eaters (which I am not). I tend to add it to sauces or devise my own dips with it; tahini is of course a principal ingredient of hummus.

Tekka *(Mitoku)*

This is another alkalising natural flavouring for soups, rice or other grains and vegetables. It is made of hatcho miso and a selection of bitter herbs, including burdock root. I love its tangy taste.

Vegetables

I receive a delivery of organic vegetables every week. I like the element of surprise in this. I receive the best that is available and build my cooking round it. My favourite vegetable is asparagus, followed closely by rocket, spinach and fresh peas (from my allotment).

Vitam-R *(Mapletons)*

This is molasses which has had the sugar fermented out of it but not the trace elements. It is kinder to the digestion than yeast extract, which it resembles in both taste and looks, and contains far less salt. I use it to make quick drinks or to flavour soups.

MAINTENANCE RECIPES

These recipes are to help you keep on the right side of your gut when you have got out of jail. Eating can be such a misery when the diet is very restricted that when we do start feeling better there is a danger of overdoing it. Resist that temptation. The following recipes should spice up your eating life considerably while keeping your gut in good shape. Feel free to adapt them. I have included ingredients which I know are appropriate to each of the three basic gut conditions. However, you may have other ideas. Do not be afraid to experiment and change the recipes to suit your requirements and taste. If you start slowly and do not eat too much, you will find out what your digestion can cope with. Also, try not to forget the basics:

- Chew thoroughly
- Do not over-eat
- Avoid the combination of starches and proteins at the same meal
- Keep up your intake of water
- Continue with the mind/body therapy you chose when you were doing the basic plan to help you remain sensitive to your gut's requirements. If you manage to stick to the basics, you will not go far wrong.

SOUPS

Spinach and Fennel Soup

Serves 4

If you suffered from diarrhoea or IBS, go easy on the onions and oil in this recipe. Instead, try softening the celery in a little stock.

> 2 tbsp olive oil
> 1 small red onion, peeled and finely chopped
> 1 stick celery, trimmed and finely chopped
> 1.2 litres (2 pt) fresh vegetable stock (see page 50)
> 2 bulbs fennel, trimmed and very thinly sliced
> 300 g (10 oz) baby spinach leaves

2 tbsp freshly chopped dill
Juice of 1 lemon
Salt and freshly ground black pepper
Natural goat's or sheep's yoghurt to serve

Heat the oil in a large saucepan and gently fry the onion and celery for 5 minutes until softened but not browned.

Pour in the stock and bring to the boil. Add the fennel, cover and simmer for 10 minutes. Add the spinach, bring to the boil, remove from the heat, cover and stand for 10 minutes.

Transfer to a blender or food processor and blend for a few seconds until smooth. Return to the saucepan, add the dill and lemon juice and adjust the seasoning. Heat through gently for 2–3 minutes until hot. Serve ladled into warm soup bowls, and top with yoghurt if preferred.

Beetroot Soup with Chives

Serves 4

This is an excellent choice for those with a tendancy towards constipation. If your system tends in the opposite direction, eat this dish sparingly.

2 tbsp olive oil
1 medium red onion, peeled and finely chopped
2 bay leaves
1 tsp caraway seeds, lightly crushed
900 ml (1^1/2 pt) fresh vegetable stock (see page 50)
225 g (8 oz) freshly cooked grated beetroot in natural juice
Salt and freshly ground black pepper
4 heaped tbsp natural goat's or sheep's yoghurt
2 tbsp freshly chopped chives
Extra caraway seeds if liked

Heat the oil in a large saucepan and gently fry the onion with the bay leaves and caraway seeds for 5 minutes until the onion is softened but not browned.

Pour in the stock, bring to the boil and stir in the beetroot. Simmer for 5 minutes. Adjust the seasoning.

Ladle into warmed soup bowls and top each portion with a tablespoon of yoghurt. Sprinkle with chives and extra caraway seeds if liked.

Note: If you prefer a smooth soup, you can blend the ingredients together.

Oriental Noodle Soup

Serves 4

If you tend towards diarrhoea or IBS, use only a small amount of ginger, and replace the cucumber with courgette.

100 g (4 oz) thin rice noodles
2 tbsp olive oil
1 bunch spring onions, trimmed, white and green parts sliced
1 garlic clove, peeled and finely chopped
2.5 cm (1 in) piece root ginger, peeled and finely grated
1.2 litres (2 pt) fresh vegetable stock (see page 50)
2 tsp Tekka seasoning
25 g (1 oz) arame
1 mini cucumber, finely shredded
100 g (4 oz) radishes, trimmed and finely shredded
2 tbsp ume plum seasoning

Place the noodles in a heatproof bowl and pour over sufficient boiling water to cover. Stand for 4 minutes, then drain well and set aside.

Meanwhile, heat the oil in a large saucepan and gently fry the spring onions, garlic and ginger for 2–3 minutes until just softened.

Pour in the stock, add the Tekka seasoning, bring to the boil and add the arame. Simmer for 3–4 minutes until tender.

Divide the noodles between four warmed soup bowls and ladle over the arame stock. Serve with the shredded vegetables seasoned with ume plum seasoning.

Spicy Winter Lentil Soup

Serves 4

Lentils usually create wind but these black lentils (urad dall) don't produce so much. This soup is good for those who tend towards constipation, but a bit too strong for those who have suffered with diarrhoea or IBS. Gormeh sabzi is a Persian chopped dried herb blend of fenugreek, chives, coriander and parsley which is found in specialist Middle Eastern supermarkets. If you prefer, you can double the amount of chopped coriander instead.

4 cardamom pods
1 tsp cumin seeds
1 tsp coriander seeds
2 tbsp olive oil
1 medium onion, peeled and finely chopped
1 garlic clove, peeled and finely chopped
1.2 litres (2 pt) fresh vegetable stock (see page 50)
100 g (4 oz) urad dall, rinsed
350 g (12 oz) parsnips, peeled and finely chopped
2 tbsp gormeh sabzi
Salt and freshly ground black pepper
2 tbsp freshly chopped coriander

In a pestle and mortar or spice grinder, lightly crush the cardamom to split the husks. Discard the husks and crush the cardamom seeds together with the cumin and coriander seeds.

Heat the oil in a large saucepan and gently fry the onion and garlic with the spices for 5 minutes until softened and fragrant.

Pour in the stock and bring to the boil. Add the urad dall, bring back to the boil, cover and simmer for 35 minutes. Stir in the parsnips and gormeh sabzi, bring back to the boil and simmer, uncovered, for a further 10–15 minutes until tender. Adjust the seasoning.

Either serve as a chunky soup, or blend for a few seconds in a food processor for a smoother result. Serve sprinkled with freshly chopped coriander.

Chilled Avocado Soup

Serves 4

This is a very nice blend if you tend towards constipation, but a bit too rich if diarrhoea is a problem.

1 medium leek
2 large ripe avocados
Juice of 1 lemon
2 tbsp olive oil
Small bunch fresh basil leaves
225 g (8 oz) natural goat's or sheep's yoghurt
600 ml (1 pt) fresh vegetable stock (see page 50)
Salt and freshly ground black pepper
Small basil leaves to garnish

Trim the leek; slice down widthways and rinse under cold running water to flush out any trapped dirt. Shake well to remove excess water. Shred finely and place in a food processor.

Peel the avocados; cut in half and discard the stones. Roughly chop the flesh and toss in the lemon juice – this will help delay discolouration. Place in the food processor along with the bunch of basil leaves, yoghurt and stock. Blend for a few seconds until smooth. Adjust the seasoning.

Place a few ice cubes in serving bowls and ladle the soup over the top. Serve sprinkled with more basil leaves and a dusting of black pepper.

Note: This soup is best prepared and served as soon as possible, otherwise it will begin to discolour.

SAUCES AND DRESSINGS

Most recipes in this section will be too rich for those suffering from diarrhoea or IBS, but used in small amounts, particularly accompanied by dill, you will be able to enjoy the wide variety of flavours these recipes offer.

Simple Olive Oil, Lemon and Herb Dressing

Makes 150 ml (¹/4 pt)

6 tbsp cold-pressed virgin olive oil
Juice of 2 lemons
Salt and freshly ground black pepper
4 tbsp freshly chopped herbs of your choice such as dill, basil,
    parsley, coriander or chives, or a combination

Mix all the ingredients together and serve tossed into non-wheat
pasta and noodles, salads and vegetables, or drizzle over fish or
chicken. Store in a sealed container in the fridge for up to 5 days.

Salsa Verde

Makes 200 ml (7 fl oz)

50 g (2 oz) can anchovy fillets in olive oil
1 garlic clove, peeled and finely chopped
Juice of 2 lemons
6 tbsp cold-pressed virgin olive oil
50 g (2 oz) pitted black olives, finely chopped
2 tbsp freshly chopped parsley
Freshly ground black pepper

Discard the oil from the anchovies and drain the fillets on
absorbent kitchen paper. Finely chop the fillets and mix together
with the remaining ingredients.

Serve with salads, vegetables and fish. Store in a sealed
container in the fridge for up to 5 days.

Rocket Pesto

Makes 300 ml (10 fl oz)

1 garlic clove, peeled
50 g (2 oz) pine nuts
150 ml (5 fl oz) cold-pressed virgin olive oil
50 g (2 oz) wild rocket leaves
15 g (^{1}/2 oz) fresh basil
50 g (2 oz) Pecorino Romano (hard sheep's milk cheese), finely
    grated
Salt and freshly ground black pepper

Place all the ingredients in a food processor or blender and blend for a few seconds until smooth and thick. Serve as a dip for vegetables, or for a topping for fish and chicken. Store in a sealed container in the fridge for up to 5 days.

Chermoula Dressing

Makes 100 ml (3^1/2 fl oz)

^{1}/2 tsp cumin seeds
1 tbsp cider vinegar
2 tbsp lemon juice
3 tbsp cold-pressed virgin olive oil
1 tsp clear honey
1 garlic clove, peeled and crushed
^{1}/2 tsp ground paprika
^{1}/2 tsp chilli powder
2 tbsp freshly chopped parsley
2 tbsp freshly chopped coriander
Salt and freshly ground black pepper

Grind the cumin seeds in a pestle and mortar or spice grinder and then mix with the remaining ingredients. Use as a marinade for white fish or chicken before roasting, or use as a dressing or dip for salads or steamed vegetables. Store in a sealed container in the fridge for up to 5 days.

Herb Mayonnaise

Makes approx. 300 ml (10 fl oz)

2 medium organic egg yolks
$1/2$ tsp Dijon mustard
$1/2$ tsp salt
250 ml (9 fl oz) cold-pressed virgin olive oil
2 tbsp lemon juice
4 tbsp freshly chopped herbs of your choice such as dill,
    parsley, coriander, basil, chives, or a combination

Place the egg yolks in a bowl and whisk in the mustard and salt using an electric whisk.

Pour the oil into a jug with a narrow spout and, drop by drop, drizzle the oil into the egg mixture whilst whisking at the same time. You must add the oil very slowly at the beginning otherwise the mayonnaise will not thicken.

Once the mixture begins to thicken, you can increase the flow of oil to a thin stream until it is all used up. Stir in the lemon juice and herbs, and adjust the seasoning if necessary. Chill for 30 minutes before serving as a dip for vegetables or as an accompaniment to grilled or roast fish or chicken. Store in a sealed container in the fridge for up to 1 week.

Vegetable and Dill Yoghurt Dressing

Makes approx. 300 ml (10 fl oz)

100 g (4 oz) cucumber, very finely chopped
50 g (2 oz) radishes, trimmed and grated
225 g (8 oz) natural sheep's milk Greek yoghurt
2 tbsp freshly chopped dill
2 tbsp cider vinegar
Salt and freshly ground black pepper

Mix all the ingredients together and season to taste. Serve as a dip for salads and vegetables, or as a lighter sauce to accompany fish or chicken instead of mayonnaise. Store in a sealed container in the fridge for up to 5 days.

Japanese Sesame Dressing

Makes approx. 125 ml (5 fl oz)

4 tbsp cold-pressed virgin olive oil
2 tbsp sesame oil
2 tbsp ume plum seasoning
2 tbsp Tamari soy sauce
2 tbsp freshly chopped chives
2 tbsp toasted sesame seeds

Mix all the ingredients together and serve with vegetables, salads, chicken or fish. Store in a sealed container in the fridge for up to 1 week.

Thai Coconut and Lemongrass Sauce

Makes approx. 300 ml (10 fl oz)

1 tbsp olive oil
2 shallots, peeled and finely chopped
1 garlic clove, peeled and finely chopped
1 small red chilli, deseeded and finely chopped (optional)
2.5 cm (1 in) piece root ginger, peeled and finely chopped
1 stalk lemon grass, trimmed and finely chopped
2 kaffir lime leaves
200 ml (7 fl oz) canned coconut milk
150 ml (5 fl oz) fresh vegetable stock (see page 50)
Pinch of salt
2 tbsp freshly chopped coriander

Heat the oil in a saucepan and gently fry the shallots, garlic, chilli, if using, root ginger and lemon grass for 5 minutes until softened and fragrant.

Tear the lime leaves slightly and add to the mixture along with the coconut milk and stock. Bring to the boil and simmer gently for 10 minutes until slightly thickened. Remove from the heat and cool for 10 minutes, then discard the lime leaves. If you prefer a smooth sauce, blend for a few seconds in a food processor.

Add salt to season and sprinkle in the chopped coriander. Serve the sauce hot or cold with noodles or rice, vegetables, chicken or fish.

MAIN DISHES

Roast Barberry Lamb

Serves 4

4 tbsp olive oil
4 bay leaves
Pinch of saffron
1.25 kg (2 lb 10 oz) half leg of organic lamb, all skin and fat
    removed
4 red onions, peeled and sliced
2 tbsp lemon juice
4 tbsp dried barberries
1 tbsp clear honey
Salt and freshly ground pepper
2 large sprigs of fresh rosemary

Preheat the oven to 180°C/350°F/Gas Mark 4. Heat the oil in a large flameproof casserole dish with a tight-fitting lid. Add the bay leaves, saffron and lamb, and seal the lamb all over for 3–4 minutes until browned. Drain the lamb, reserving the fat and juices.

Gently fry the onions with the lemon juice for 4–5 minutes in the casserole dish until softened, then add the barberries and honey, and cook for a further minute. Season. Replace the lamb in the dish and lay the rosemary on top.

Cover the top of the casserole with a layer of foil and then place the lid on top. Bake on a low shelf in the oven, undisturbed for $2^1/2$ hours until the lamb is very tender and collapsed away from the bone. Discard the bay leaves and woody stems from the rosemary.

Serve the lamb meat with the onion and barberry mixture, accompanied with freshly cooked green beans or broccoli.

Baked Lamb with Fennel

Serves 4

If you tend towards diarrhoea or IBS, use onion and olive oil sparingly, and have only a small portion of lamb until your digestion has completely settled.

1 medium red onion, peeled and sliced
2 fennel bulbs, trimmed and cut into thick wedges
4 x 100 g (4 oz) lean boneless organic lamb steaks, trimmed
1 tbsp olive oil
1 tbsp lemon juice
1 garlic clove, peeled and finely chopped
Salt and freshly ground black pepper
2 tbsp freshly chopped parsley

Preheat the oven to 180°C/350°F/Gas Mark 4. Lay the red onion
and fennel in the base of a casserole dish, and top with the lamb
steaks.

Mix the remaining ingredients together, except the parsley,
and pour over the lamb and vegetables. Cover and stand for 30
minutes.

Gently mix the vegetables and lamb together, then cover and
bake in the oven for 1 hour. Remove the lid and cook for a further
10 minutes until lightly brown and tender. Serve the lamb and
fennel sprinkled with parsley and accompanied by freshly cooked
green vegetables.

Saffron and Lemon Baked Chicken

For those with a tendency towards diarrhoea or IBS, leave out the
garlic and bay leaves from this recipe and replace the artichokes
with thinly sliced courgette.

Serves 4

2 tbsp olive oil
4 x 350 g (12 oz) organic chicken portions, skinned
8 whole, unpeeled, garlic cloves
150 ml (5 fl oz) fresh chicken stock (see page 50)
Large pinch of saffron
4 bay leaves
Salt and freshly ground black pepper
400 g (14 oz) can artichoke hearts, drained, rinsed and halved

75 g (3 oz) pitted black olives
Finely grated rind and juice of 1 lemon
1 tbsp clear honey
2 tbsp freshly chopped parsley
1 lemon, cut into wedges

Preheat the oven to 190°C/375°F/Gas Mark 5. Heat the oil in a flameproof casserole dish with a tight-fitting lid and seal the chicken with the garlic for 3–4 minutes, turning until lightly golden all over.

Pour in the stock and add the saffron, bay leaves and seasoning. Bring to the boil, then cover and transfer to the oven to bake for 40 minutes.

Stir in the artichoke hearts, olives and lemon rind and juice, replace the lid and continue to cook uncovered for a further 10 minutes. Discard the bay leaves, and the garlic cloves if preferred.

Add honey to taste, and serve the chicken with its vegetables and juices, sprinkled with chopped parsley and accompanied by freshly cooked green vegetables, and wedges of lemon to squeeze over.

Steamed Chicken with Summer Vegetables

Serves 4

A good recipe for all conditions.

4 x 150 g (5 oz) boneless, skinless organic chicken breasts
Salt and freshly ground black pepper
4 bay leaves
Juice and finely grated rind of 1 lemon
100 g (4 oz) fine asparagus tips, trimmed
100 g (4 oz) fine green beans, topped and tailed
100 g (4 oz) sugar snap peas, topped and tailed
1 large leek, trimmed, rinsed and shredded
4 tbsp freshly chopped dill

Wash and pat dry the chicken breasts using absorbent kitchen paper. Season on both sides, and arrange in the bottom of a large steaming compartment, large sieve or colander lined with baking parchment. Arrange a bay leaf on top of each chicken breast and sprinkle with half the lemon juice, and all the rind.

Bring a large saucepan of water to the boil, place the steamer over the water, cover and steam for 20 minutes. Remove the steamer, and lift out the chicken. Arrange the vegetables in the steamer and place the chicken on top. Sprinkle with remaining lemon juice, replace on the saucepan, cover and cook for a further 7–8 minutes until tender and cooked through. Discard the bay leaves.

Drain the chicken and vegetables and serve each portion sprinkled with chopped dill.

Baked Salmon and Asparagus

Serves 4

Reduce the olive oil in this recipe if you have a tendency towards diarrhoea or IBS, and replace the salmon with firm white fish such as cod or halibut

675 g (1¹/2 lb) young asparagus spears
1 tsp coarse sea salt
4 x 150 g (5 oz) thick skinless organic salmon fillets
Freshly ground black pepper
3 tbsp olive oil
2 tbsp freshly chopped dill
1 lemon, cut into wedges

Preheat the oven to 200°C/400°F/Gas Mark 6. Trim away approx. 4 cm (1¹/2 in) of the woody ends from the asparagus, then lay side by side in a small, shallow roasting tin. Sprinkle with sea salt.

Wash and pat dry the salmon fillets with absorbent kitchen paper and lay on top of the asparagus. Season with freshly ground black pepper.

Drizzle all over with the olive oil and bake in the oven for 30 minutes until tender and cooked through. Drain and serve sprinkled with freshly chopped dill and wedges of lemon to squeeze over. Ideal accompanied with Salsa Verde (see page 77).

Salmon Florentine

Serves 4

Choose firm white fish fillets such as cod or halibut for this recipe if you tend towards diarrhoea or IBS.

4 x 150 g (5 oz) tail-end skinless organic salmon fillets
Freshly ground black pepper
150 ml (5 fl oz) dry white wine
Juice of 1 lemon
2 bay leaves
1 tbsp olive oil
450 g (1 lb) baby spinach leaves, washed and trimmed
Pinch of salt
$1/2$ tsp ground nutmeg
4 tbsp natural goat's or sheep's milk yoghurt
2 tbsp freshly chopped dill
1 lemon, cut into wedges

Wash and pat dry the salmon fillets using absorbent kitchen paper. Season on both sides with black pepper and place in a shallow pan with a lid. Pour in the wine and lemon juice, and add the bay leaves. Bring to the boil, cover and simmer gently for 7–8 minutes until tender and cooked through.

Meanwhile, heat the oil in a large frying pan and stir-fry the spinach for 2–3 minutes until just wilted. Remove from the heat, season with salt and nutmeg. Mix in the yoghurt.

To serve, pile the spinach mixture on to warmed serving plates. Drain the salmon and place on top of the spinach. Sprinkle with dill and serve with wedges of lemon to squeeze over.

Tip

This is the perfect way to poach salmon for any dish. If you want to serve cold salmon, simply leave to cool in the cooking liquid, drain, chill and serve with your choice of dressing or sauce.

Simple Crab and Avocado Salad

Serves 4

A good recipe for those with a tendency towards constipation, but not for the diarrhoea sufferer. If you have had IBS, and are feeling more well-tuned, then you can try a smaller amount.

> 2 large ripe avocados
> 100 g (4 oz) rocket leaves
> 2 x 190 g tins white crab meat, well drained
> 1 quantity of Simple Olive Oil, Lemon and Herb Dressing, made
>   with fresh dill (see page 77)
> 1 lemon, cut into wedges

Just before serving, peel the skin from the avocados. Cut in half and remove the stones. Then slice each avocado thickly.

Arrange the rocket leaves on serving plates and top with a few slices of avocado slices and a pile of crab meat. Sprinkle with dressing and serve immediately accompanied with lemon wedges to squeeze over.

Fish and Papaya Salad

Serves 4

Use only white fish for this recipe if you have had diarrhoea or IBS. Cut down on the olive oil, and leave out the onion and chilli.

> 2 x 150 g (5 oz) thick, skinless organic salmon fillets
> 2 x 150 g (5 oz) thick skinless cod fillets
> Freshly ground black pepper
> 150 ml (5 fl oz) dry white wine
> Juice of 1 lemon
> 2 bay leaves
> 1 large ripe papaya
> Finely grated rind and juice of 1 lime
> 1 small red onion, peeled and finely sliced (optional)
> 1 small red chilli, deseeded and finely chopped (optional)
> 2 tbsp cold-pressed virgin olive oil

4 tbsp freshly chopped parsley
2 limes, cut into wedges

Wash and pat dry the fish fillets using absorbent kitchen paper. Season on both sides with black pepper and place in a shallow pan with a lid. Pour in the wine and lemon juice. Add the bay leaves. Bring to the boil, cover and simmer gently for 8–10 minutes until just tender. Remove from the heat and allow to cool in the cooking liquid. Drain, cover and chill for 30 minutes.

Meanwhile, peel the papaya. Cut in half and scoop out the seeds. Chop the flesh into bite-sized pieces and place in a bowl. Toss in the lime rind and juice. Cover and chill until required.

Just before serving, flake the fish into bite-sized pieces and gently mix into the papaya along with the onion and chilli, if using.

Pile on to serving plates and drizzle with olive oil. Sprinkle with chopped parsley and serve with wedges of lime to squeeze over.

Cauliflower and Broccoli Gratin

Serves 4

Cut down on the cheese or omit altogether if you have had diarrhoea or IBS.

Salt and freshly ground black pepper
350 g (12 oz) cauliflower, broken into small florets
350g (12 oz) broccoli, broken into small florets
600 g (1 lb 5 oz) natural sheep's milk Greek yoghurt
Juice and finely grated rind of 1 lemon
2 large organic egg yolks
2 tbsp freshly chopped chives
25 g (1 oz) oatbran
50 g (2 oz) Pecorino Romano (hard sheep's milk cheese), coarsely grated
2 tbsp freshly chopped parsley

Preheat the oven to 190°C/375°F/Gas Mark 5. Bring a large pan of lightly salted water to the boil and add the cauliflower and broccoli. Bring back to the boil, cover and cook for 2 minutes. Drain well and arrange in a shallow ovenproof dish.

Mix the yoghurt with plenty of seasoning, the lemon rind and juice, egg yolks and chives, then pour over the vegetables. Sprinkle with oatbran and the cheese on top. Bake in the oven for 40–45 minutes or until set and lightly golden. Serve sprinkled with chopped parsley.

Iranian-style Pilaf

Serves 4

Use less of the spices in this recipe if you have had diarrhoea or IBS. As on page 75, you can substitute the gormeh sabzi with fresh herbs.

Salt and freshly ground black pepper
250 g (9 oz) thin green beans, topped, tailed and cut into short
    lengths
2 tbsp olive oil
1 medium red onion, peeled and chopped
Juice of 1 lemon
2 bay leaves
Pinch of saffron
1 tsp coriander seeds, crushed
1 tsp cumin seeds, crushed
4 cardamom pods, lightly crushed
450 g (1 lb) cooked basmati rice (see page 56)
4 tbsp gormeh sabzi
50 g (2 oz) whole almonds, slivered

Bring a small saucepan of lightly salted water to the boil, add the beans, cover and cook or 4–5 minutes until just cooked. Drain well, reserving the cooking water.

Heat the oil in a large frying pan or wok and stir-fry the onion with a little of the lemon juice, the bay leaves and spices for 3–4 minutes until softened.

Stir in the rice and gormeh sabzi and stir-fry for a further 2–3 minutes. Add the beans and 4 tablespoons reserved cooking liquid. Stir-fry for 2 minutes until hot and thoroughly mixed. Discard the bay leaves and cardamom pods. Adjust the seasoning.

Sprinkle over remaining lemon juice and the almonds to serve.

Pasta with Pine Nuts, Lemon and Rocket

Serves 4

Use less lemon, garlic and chilli in this recipe if you have an upset stomach.

Salt and freshly ground black pepper
450 g (1 lb) buckwheat spaghetti
2 tbsp cold-pressed virgin olive oil
Finely grated rind of 1 lemon
2 tbsp lemon juice
1 garlic clove, peeled and crushed (optional)
1 small red chilli, deseeded and finely chopped (optional)
75 g (3 oz) wild rocket leaves
75 g (3 oz) pitted black olives, chopped
50 g (2 oz) toasted pine nuts

Bring a large saucepan of lightly salted water to the boil and cook the spaghetti according to the packet instructions. Drain well and return to the saucepan.

Meanwhile, mix together the olive oil, lemon rind and juice, and the garlic and chilli, if using.

Once the spaghetti is cooked, return it to a low heat and stir in the dressing. Add the rocket leaves and chopped olives, and cook, stirring gently, for 3–4 minutes until the rocket has wilted. Adjust the seasoning.

Pile into warmed serving bowls and serve sprinkled with toasted pine nuts. Serve with freshly cooked steamed vegetables.

PUDDINGS

Baked Pears with Lemon and Maple Syrup

Serves 4

If you suffer from wind, only have this dish as a treat and not straight after other food. Eat it later on in the day

4 large ripe pears
Finely grated rind and juice of 1 lemon
4 cardamom pods
25 g (1 oz) butter
2 tbsp maple syrup

Preheat the oven to 180°C/350°F/Gas Mark 4. Wash the pears, then core them and cut them in quarters – peel the pears if preferred. Arrange them in a shallow ovenproof dish and sprinkle with lemon juice and rind.

Lightly crush the cardamom pods, and remove the seeds. Discard the husks, and crush the seeds, then sprinkle over the pears.

Melt the butter with the maple syrup and drizzle over the pears. Cover with foil and bake for 25 minutes until tender. Remove the foil and cook for a further 5 minutes. Serve hot or cold with the cooking juices, accompanied with natural goat's or sheep's yoghurt.

Spiced Apple Crumble

Serves 4–6

As before, if you suffer from wind only have this dish as a treat and not straight after other food.

675 g (1^1/2 lb) green dessert apples
Juice and rind of 1 lemon
1 tsp ground cinnamon
^{1}/4 tsp ground cloves
175 g (6 oz) oatbran
50 g (2 oz) ground almonds
50 g (2 oz) butter, softened
2 tbsp maple syrup

Preheat the oven to 190°C/375°F/Gas Mark 5. Wash and core the apples. Halve and then slice very thinly. Place in a bowl and toss in the lemon juice and rind and the spices. Then pile into an 1.5 litres (2^1/2 pt) oval ovenproof pie dish.

In a bowl, mix the oatbran and ground almonds together. Rub in the butter until well mixed and crumbly, and stir in the maple syrup. Spoon the mixture over the apples and bake in the oven for 30–40 minutes until golden, tender and cooked through.

Speedy Berry and Banana Yoghurt Ice

Serves 4

Serve as a treat on its own and eat very slowly, to reduce the risk of the bananas fermenting

    1 large banana
    225 g (8 oz) assorted prepared small berries such as raspberries,
        blueberries, blackberries and small strawberries
    300 g (10 oz) natural live sheep's milk yoghurt
    1 tbsp organic clear honey

Peel and chop the banana into small pieces and arrange on a tray lined with baking parchment. Wash and pat dry the berries and arrange on the tray with the banana. Open freeze for 45 minutes or until frozen and firm.

Just before serving transfer the frozen fruit to a food processor and add the yoghurt. Blend for a few seconds until icy, creamy and smooth. Sweeten with honey to taste and serve immediately.

Speedy Melon Sorbet

Serves 4

    900 g (2 lb) wedge watermelon
    Finely grated rind and juice of 2 limes
    3–4 tsp orange flower water
    1/4 tsp ground cinnamon

Slice off the skin from the melon and discard the seeds. Chop the flesh into small pieces and arrange on a tray lined with baking parchment. Place in the freezer for about 1 hour or until frozen and firm.

Just before serving, transfer the frozen melon to a food processor. Add the lime juice and rind and blend for a few seconds until icy and smooth.

Serve immediately sprinkled with orange flower water and a little cinnamon.

Middle Eastern Fruit Compote

Serves 4

A good choice if you tend towards constipation, but not advisable if you have had diarrhoea or IBS.

100 g (4 oz) hunza dried apricots
100 g (4 oz) unsulphured dried peaches
100 g (4 oz) prunes
50 g (2 oz) unsulphured dried pears
50 g (2 oz) unsulphured dried apples
450 ml (16 fl oz) unsweetened organic apple juice
6 cardamom pods
6 cloves
1 cinnamon stick, broken
2 tbsp rosewater
25 g (1 oz) natural pistachio nuts, chopped

Place all the dried fruits in a saucepan with the apple juice. Add the spices and bring to the boil. Simmer for 10–15 minutes until plump and tender. Allow to cool, then transfer to a dish, cover and chill for 30 minutes.

Just before serving, discard the spices, and sprinkle with the rosewater and chopped pistachios. Serve accompanied with goat or sheep's milk yoghurt.

Tip

You can serve this compote hot if you prefer. Simply cool for 10 minutes, then discard the spices and serve whilst still warm.

Vanilla Custard

Serves 4

The perfect treat for an upset stomach; it is very comforting and reassuring.

600 ml (20 fl oz) goat or sheep's milk
1 vanilla pod
$2^{1}/_{2}$ tbsp crushed kudzo starch or $1^{1}/_{2}$ tbsp arrowroot
2 tbsp maple syrup

Pour all but 3 tablespoons of the milk into a saucepan. Split the vanilla pod lengthwise and scrape out the seeds into the saucepan. Add the pod and bring just to below boiling point. Remove from the heat and stand for 30 minutes. Discard the pod.

Blend the kudzo starch or arrowroot with the reserved milk and stir into the vanilla milk. Heat gently, stirring until boiling, then simmer, stirring, for 1–2 minutes, until thickened.

Stir in maple syrup to sweeten, and serve hot or cold, with fruit if liked.

Tip
If preferred, replace the vanilla pod with 1 teaspoon of good quality vanilla essence. Simply stir into the custard along with the maple syrup – you don't need to heat the milk first.

Coconut Custard

Serves 4

As vanilla custard, the perfect treat for an upset stomach.

300 ml (10 fl oz) goat or sheep's milk
300 ml (10 fl oz) canned coconut milk
1 cinnamon stick, broken
$1/4$ tsp freshly grated nutmeg
4 cardamom pods, lightly crushed
$2^{1}/_{2}$ tbsp crushed kudzo starch or $1^{1}/_{2}$ tbsp arrowroot
2–3 tbsp maple syrup

Pour all but 3 tablespoons of the milk into a saucepan. Add the spices and bring to just below boiling point. Remove from the heat and stand for 30 minutes. Discard the cinnamon and cardamom-pods.

Blend the kudzo starch or arrowroot with the reserved milk and stir into the spiced milk. Heat gently, stirring until boiling, then simmer, stirring, for 1–2 minutes until thickened.

Stir in maple syrup to taste, and serve hot or cold, with fruit if liked.

Feeding the Future

When I was growing up in Sweden I used to hate a particular kind of bun which it was traditional to have in the afternoon. This foul-tasting concoction had to be eaten before we were allowed the delicious cake that followed, the point presumably being to instil the idea of forbearance always taking precedence over pleasure. The tactic was lost on me. I would stuff my bun into the deepest recesses of the nearest piece of furniture and then present myself for the food I really liked. In the same way, I cannot abide cooked carrots because my mother told me that I would not be allowed pudding if I did not eat them. If my own experience is any guide, there is a danger of fostering in children negative associations with certain foods and repeating the mistakes our parents made with us. How many adults can honestly say that the manipulation and bribery their parents used to get them to eat a pile of soggy greens or some such culinary horror did other than stiffen their resistance to that food in later life?

If food is to be enjoyed from the cradle, it has to be made enjoyable – and not just the food itself but the experience of eating. It is a great pity that comparatively few families these days regularly sit down together for meals. These occasions provide opportunities to develop in children the notion of food as a pleasure, a taste adventure. Most small children will take an interest in what Daddy and Mummy are eating – they want to be grown-up and try what is on offer. The table can become a place that is central to their experience of growing up, of appreciating different flavours and developing familial relationships. It may be difficult for you to provide this every day, but even if it is only at weekends your child will benefit. Children who eat on their own without the stimulus of adult company tend to regard food in a rather detached manner, as something they must do before they are allowed to play or watch television.

Being positive about food will encourage your child to do the same. This will require giving it your time and attention; when you have finished eating, try not to get up immediately. Everyone's digestion benefits from resting after a meal. Children take their cue from adults and if the routine is to clear the table and then race off to do something else, they will do the same. I encourage my small patients to get into the habit of telling each other or their parents funny stories. Under the rules of this game, everyone at the table has to tell an amusing story and get everyone else to laugh. Often the amusement is in the telling and interplay rather than the stories themselves, but this does not matter. The aim is to get everyone to loosen up and forget about 'doing'. Relaxing is the best digestive there is.

Food can be exciting and the earlier children are introduced to this concept the broader and more adventurous their tastes in food will be. Of course there will be dishes or ingredients they will not like – despite the loud, approving noises you make to persuade them to the contrary – and these reservations should be respected. Rather than applying strict rules, it is far better to encourage a child to eat a few mouthfuls of greens or whatever food it finds unpalatable and leave it at that. Meal times should not become stressful occasions with certain foods at the centre of a battle of wills. Our tastes change and sometimes children will learn to appreciate foods they once found difficult. Explore with the child different ways of preparing the offending food to see if you cannot make it more appealing. If this does not succeed, just accept that we cannot all like the same foods and try something else. Where vegetables are concerned, there are so many to choose from that wholesome alternatives should not be difficult to find. Most children I know like the 'baby' varieties, such as mange-tout, corn, sugar snap peas – and it is rare for them to dislike raw carrots. Seasonal fruits, frozen yoghurts and fruit purées are generally well liked. Just as when you choose and cook for yourself, look around, try new things to interest your child.

Once children are old enough to eat solids it is a good idea to view their diet as a simplified version of your own, although the rule about not consuming starches and proteins at the same meal does not apply. Happily, at their age, having enough of the right enzymes is not a problem. However, the guides about the amount of food and chewing are relevant. Even for a child with a good appetite a huge plateful of food can be off-putting. Give modest portions and let the child ask for more if he or she is still hungry. One can make chewing fun, not just a command, by doing it too.

Childhood Legacies

Every baby carries a legacy from its ancestors, and especially its mother. If a mother has not looked after her digestive system, her baby will tend to be weak in this department. The tendency will show itself in windiness or pain as the child grows older. Often a dislike of certain foods is directly related to the discomfort they cause rather than their taste. Frequent bouts of colic or wind indicate that the child is not digesting well and especial care should be taken with the diet; it may be necessary to add a suitable Acidophilus formula (see page 138) to the child's food. Look closely at the kind and quantity of starches in the diet: is there a preponderance of simple carbohydrates (soft drinks, crisps, biscuits, sugared breakfast cereals, etc)?

The main cause of digestive problems in children is over-consumption of wheat and foods that send the blood sugar level into overdrive. A packet of crisps or a snack bar may seem like an innocuous filler to last them until you get them home for tea but it is the type of food that gets the body into the habit of 'swinging'. By the time the child gets home he will probably be in the down phase of the cycle and not feeling like doing his homework. Low blood sugar types are invariably made, not born.

The easiest way to avoid the danger of low blood sugar is to make a few simple adjustments. Substitute oat-based products for wheat-based products and honey or fructose for sugar. Try to introduce interesting fruit and vegetables, wheat-free pastas and breads. Windy children, especially, should feel the benefit of being given sourdough rye bread, which has been fermented and is easier to digest, instead of bread made with wheat. Cow's milk can also be problematic and should be eliminated from the diet of children who produce a lot of mucus; give them goat's milk (or even ewe's) instead.

Many children suffer constipation in silence. This is hardly surprising given the unwillingness of most adults to discuss it. Once a child is out of nappies, all talk of bowel movements and interest in them stops. Children need to be helped to get into a pattern with their bowel movements. This will happen if they are given time in the mornings and are not rushed into blocking them. Rushing induces stress which is the most potent cause of constipation there is. Children can get into the habit of 'holding on' – leaving for school comes at the wrong time for them or they do not feel comfortable about going to the lavatory at school. Such a simple process can become needlessly fraught with difficulty and result in a tense, discomforted child. Look for unmistakeable signs of bad fermentation: a bloated stomach with wind accompaniment.

If your child eats early in the evening, around five or six o'clock, it is beneficial for him to have a few stewed apricots or prunes with goat's yoghurt and honey before bedtime. This will ensure that the blood sugar remains even throughout the night; nightmares are often a sign of a drop. The constipated child will also benefit from this regime. Cal-M (see page 139) at bedtime will soothe the nervous system and the muscles, aiding sleep.

Choosing Foods

These days the choice of foods is vast, even in supermarkets, and you are bound to find healthy alternatives that your child enjoys. Sometimes the mothers of children for whom I recommend dietary changes worry that by denying them foods they like they are in effect depriving them of love. The children themselves are usually more than happy to try something different and in comparison with their mothers are quite matter-of-fact and sensible about the changes, which in most cases are small. With a little thought and care children can be encouraged into adopting good eating habits that will last them a lifetime – and ensure they have a healthy digestive system.

Let us start with the first meal of the day.

Breakfast
Some children will readily eat my oatbran porridge recipe (see page 49) and it does give them a nutritious start. However, if time is tight or the porridge is not well liked, there are several prepared cereals which I can recommend:

Crusto Quinoa Crunch
Biona Organic Honey and Hazelnut Crunch
Nature's Path Millet and Rice Oatbran Flake (sweetened with
     organic fruit juice)
Wheat-free toast with pure fruit spread

Goat's, sheep's, soya or rice milk are good alternatives to cow's milk to add to these cereals. Let your child try them all and discover which one (or ones) he likes. These alternatives can also be used in hot drinks. Some children like a little Provamel Soya Dream or Image Foods Rice Dream on their oatbran porridge. If the child dislikes these alternatives, use cow's yoghurt in preference to milk because it has at least been fermented and is thus more digestible.

Packed lunches
These are a nightmare for most mothers, especially ones who are anxious to do the 'right thing' on the one hand and please their child on the other. No child likes to be sent to school with a lunch box packed with strange foodstuffs that are going to single him out as weird. Here are a few ideas which my young clients have tried and enjoyed.

1. Organic carrot strips and cucumber
   Strips of cold chicken
   Piece of fresh fruit
   Pot of fruit yoghurt; find one that your child likes, alternatively
        you can use plain yoghurt and add fresh fruit to it
   Natural Mineral Water or juice diluted with Natural Mineral
        Water

2. Organic cold sausages
   Baby tomatoes and celery sticks
   Piece of fresh fruit (not an orange)
   Piece of wheat-free flapjack
   Natural Mineral Water or juice diluted with Natural Mineral
        Water

3. Sandwich made from gluten-free bread; many types are available but I find the Village Bakery range offers the widest choice
   Filling: Almond butter (see page 104 for important note about this product) or Suma Mushroom pâté or Vitam-R (similar to yeast extract but less salty – see page 71)
   A tub of salad or vegetables
   Piece of fresh fruit
   Small fruit bar
   Natural Mineral Water or juice diluted with Natural Mineral Water

4. Cheese mixed with diced cucumber and celery and grated carrot and apple
   Wheat-free bread roll
   Piece of fresh fruit
   Small packet of organic raisins
   Natural Mineral Water or juice diluted with Natural Mineral Water

5. Pot of cold, wheat-free pasta salad
   Carrot sticks
   Piece of fresh fruit
   Natural Mineral Water or juice diluted with Natural Mineral Water

6. Vegetable or chicken stock (use recipes on pages 49–51 to devise your own soup)
   Piece of fresh fruit
   Small fruit bar
   Natural Mineral Water or juice diluted with Natural Mineral Water

Food Tips

● Instead of giving your child sweets after school, give him or her fruit. If you collect your child by car, take a small pot of stewed fruit with a little Udo's Oil or Missing Link mixed in. This should not be too much of a chore, especially as you may well be doing the same for yourself. If your child travels by bus or train, or is collected by somebody else, make sure he has an apple and an organic fruit bar for the journey home.

- Often children only drink when they are very thirsty because they are busy doing more exciting things. It is important – especially for the constipated child – that they acquire the habit of drinking enough water. You can help by telling them why it is important. Still Natural Mineral Water is an ideal drink for them. For a change, occasionally add some unsweetened fruit concentrate. This contains none of the synthetic sweeteners which are widely used in drinks for children (see flavoured waters on pages 128–9). There are other brands which do not use such additives – seek them out and see which ones your child likes.

- Use baked potatoes instead of chips, and in preference to mashed potatoes. Cooking potatoes in their skins will force your child to chew and thus reduce the generally high glucose response potatoes usually elicit.

- Snack bars and crisps are high in the wrong fats, sugar, salt and additives. Try to keep your child's consumption of them to a minimum. Some alternatives to the main brands are marginally healthier. Try the following (if some of these packets offer too much for one snack, divide their contents between several bags):

  > Brown rice crackers (Wakama)
  > Vegetable Roots (Cottage Delight)
  > Tortilla Chips (Apache)
  > Grizzly Fruit Bars
  > Kettle Valley Fruit Snacks
  > Allos Fruit and Nut Bars
  > Shepherd Boy Fruit and Nut Bars
  > Allos Trophy Bars

- I use fructose as an alternative to sugar in cooking and to add to foods that are too bitter without; fructose is available from most chemists, health food shops and high quality supermarkets. Maple syrup and a good organic honey are other sound alternatives to refined cane sugar. Oligo-fibre may also be used as a sweetener, and I often suggest it for children with constipation, because it encourages the right bacterial flora to grow. If you use the Oligofibre for constipation, start slowly – too much too quickly will give the child wind.

- The proteins in cow's products are less digestible than those found in goat's or even sheep's milk, which is why I suggest keeping them to a minimum in the diet. Additional alternatives to cow's milk are rice and soya milk. Try putting Provamel Soya Dream or Image Foods Rice Dream instead of cream on fruit or in the dishes you cook. Some children like these on their oatbran porridge, too.

- Look for a wheat-free organic tomato ketchup, such as Life and Health brand.

Chapter Seven

A–Zs of Opportunity

Here is your opportunity to mix and match a selection of common ingredients and herbs to fit your requirements. All of them will be familiar to you and most of them you would probably think should form part of a broad-based, nutritionally rich diet. In a number of cases, however, you will find that lots of vitamins and minerals do not necessarily ensure that a food is appropriate for everyone in all circumstances.

I have tried to give a profile of each of the foods in terms of what they offer and how they may help or hinder you health-wise. Hopefully you should be able to find favourite foods and see how these fit with the state you are in. If you find that a number of foods seem to be out of bounds, do not despair. Unless you are falling off the end of the degeneration curve, it is highly unlikely that many – if any – of your favourite foods will be out of bounds for long. Remember: whatever food you eat, you can transform it and take measures to render it more gut friendly.

When you have discovered which foods you would do better to avoid and which to become better acquainted with, start experimenting and searching out new tastes and taste patterns.

And whatever you choose to eat – enjoy it!

Food

Alcohol

The alcoholic content is often held up as the yardstick by which to judge whether certain alcoholic drinks are good or bad. Would that the subject were this simple. Taken in moderation (1–2 tots a day), high-proof spirits, such as brandy, whisky, gin and vodka, are unlikely to cause a deterioration in the basically healthy person. Too much of any alcohol, however, no matter its alcoholic content, is injurious to health because it robs our bodies of the vitamins and minerals needed to keep us well. Indeed, it is the seemingly innocuous that can be most dangerous. The best example of this is beer, probably the least benign of all alcoholic drinks.

The practice of making beer with carcinogens such as nitrosamines should give the health-conscious pause for thought. In my experience beer ferments too much and should certainly be avoided by those with ulcers, heartburn or other stomach problems in whom it stimulates the production of excess acid. The beer-lover with no gastric problems would be wise to choose one uncontaminated by chemical additives and limit his or her intake.

The acid in white wine tends to irritate the lining of the gut and should be avoided by those with delicate stomachs. It is also likely to have had chemicals included during its preparation. If you like white wine, try one that has been produced by organic means. Red wine is less acid-forming than white, although it has a bad reputation as an instigator of migraines in susceptible people, in whom it heats and over-works the liver (as do other common migraine 'triggers' such as chocolate, cheese or wheat). However, for those of us who are not susceptible, a glass or two with a meal does no harm. For what to do after those very rare occasions when you had so many that you lost count, see page 143.

Alfalfa

This plant contains almost every nutrient known to man, including live enzymes (which break down fat, cellulose and starch), and chlorophyll, which aids in the healing of a wide range of disorders, from bleeding gums to cancer. It is a tonic for the digestive and immune systems, strengthening the intestines, stomach and spleen, and is a helpful addition to the diets of those suffering with arthritis, rheumatism or peptic ulcers. Eat it sprouted or grow it in a pot and harvest it as a green.

Almond

Almonds are rich in zinc, magnesium, potassium, iron, calcium and some B vitamins, but they also contain high levels of oxalic and phytic acids which encourage the body to eliminate them, so it is unwise to eat large amounts. To ensure that the body absorbs their mineral and vitamin content, always eat them with foods that are good sources of Vitamin C. The digestive, respiratory (especially coughs and asthma) and urinary processes all benefit from almonds, as do the nerves. The fat or oil in almonds – which is virtually identical chemically to that found in olive oil – is well tolerated, even by those with liver or pancreatic difficulties; a purée made from almonds is especially recommended for them because it is nutritious and easy to digest. Even for people without these difficulties it is advisable to get into the habit of soaking whole almonds about 12 hours before you intend eating them. This process softens them, making them easier to digest and less likely to have a sandpaper effect on the gut lining.

Almond butter is a protein-rich substitute for peanut butter and thus a good alternative for those who are allergic to peanuts. However, when choosing a brand, ensure that the manufacturer is not also processing foods made with peanuts, as the product may not be free from contamination.

Apple

There are several constituents, possibly more, which give the apple its value as an all-round health food: pectin, malic and tartaric acids, quercetin and modest amounts of Vitamins A and C, B vitamins, calcium, magnesium, copper, selenium and zinc. The fibre pectin, found in the skin, lowers cholesterol levels and removes toxins; and the acids reduce the bad effects on the digestion of rich foods. Bad breath, diarrhoea, obesity and rheumatism are helped by the cleansing action of apple.

Apricot

Like broccoli, carrots and spinach, apricots are full of beta-carotene, a branch of the A family of vitamins, widely regarded as a potent protection against cancer. Fresh they should be eaten with care (see Stone fruit), and when buying them dried be sure to avoid fruits that have had their colour preserved by means of sulphur dioxide.

Artichoke (globe)

The considerable medicinal benefits offered by the artichoke reside mainly in its stem and leaves; however, the globes, too, have curative powers. Studies have shown that artichoke has a beneficial effect on cholesterol levels and on the liver and thus is a valuable food for those suffering with jaundice, and heart, circulatory and acid conditions (for example, arthritis). Artichoke is also an appetite stimulant, which is why it is so often found on menus as a starter.

Asparagus

A good source of the Vitamins A, C, B_6, folic acid and the minerals sulphur and potassium, asparagus increases faecal bulk and the rate of production of urine, and offers protection against raised cholesterol levels. Gout sufferers and those with inflamed kidneys should avoid asparagus, however, because it is high in purines and therefore acid-forming. The healthy should eat only small amounts of it. A very old French 'spring-clean' salad after the winter incorporates asparagus, celery and spinach combined with any other green herbs and vegetables.

Aubergine (eggplant)

This native of India contains glycoalkaloids which have been used in the treatment of minor skin cancers, such as basal cell carcinoma (rodent ulcer). The aubergine also has anti-bacterial and diuretic properties. In some individuals, though, it may cause pain and discomfort because of the presence of a toxin called sotanine, which interferes with enzymes in the muscles.

Avocado

An abundant source of antioxidant Vitamins A, C, E, and potassium. A mono-unsaturated fat in avocado offers protection against circulatory disorders. Substances found in the pulp of the fruit give solid evidence for its reputation as a skin rejuvenator. Other substances investigated confirm that it is also anti-bacterial and anti-fungal. A complete food, in that it contains protein and starch as well as fats, avocado is particularly alkali-forming and keeps the glucose level very even, so is excellent for low blood sugar.

Banana

Particularly high in potassium, which all the cells in our body require for proper functioning, bananas also contain zinc, iron, folic acid, calcium and Vitamin B_6. The pectin in the fruit binds to toxins and facilitates their elimination. Ripe bananas have a reputation for being beneficial if the digestion is out of kilter, either with constipation or diarrhoea. However, they can give you indigestion if your body's production of stomach acid is low. Usually I will leave them out of the diet in the initial stage of treatment because they are so difficult to chew thoroughly enough to digest. If they make you windy, your system is not coping with them well enough. If this is your experience, try mashing them with fresh lemon juice; I find this helps.

Barley

One of the oldest cultivated grains, barley can be bought as pearl barley or pot barley. The latter form is preferable because it is unpolished and has had only its indigestible outer husk removed. Barley is rich in minerals, including calcium and potassium, and contains significant amounts of B-complex vitamins. As a healing aid it is particularly valued for its anti-inflammatory effects – especially on the digestive and urinary tracts. Barley has traditionally been used for soothing irritated tissue, particularly the mucous membranes in the throat and stomach. Barley water has long been a traditional remedy for cystitis and constipation. As with oats, rye and other grains with a low gluten content, it has cholesterol-lowering properties.

Beetroot

The cancer-fighting properties that have long been associated with beetroot are thought to derive from its red pigment, beta-cyanin, which researchers believe may increase the ability of cells to absorb oxygen. A rich source of Vitamins A and C, folic acid, iron, calcium, potassium, copper, manganese, magnesium and phosphorus, beetroot is also used successfully to treat anaemia and immune system disorders. The efficacy of beetroot is increased by eating it raw. I often drink a small glass of beetroot juice before a meal to perk up the liver.

Bilberry (blaeberry, huckleberry, whortleberry)

An excellent source of Vitamin A, bilberries – in common with other berries – can help rectify problems with the liver and pancreas. Bilberries inhibit the growth of 'unfriendly' bacteria in the gut and are effective as an intestinal cleanser, appetite stimulant and regulator of the bowels. Use with caution initially, because the berries can have the effect of producing diarrhoea in some people and stopping it in others – try them in combination with grated apple. Bilberry juice can be used to soothe inflamed gums and as a gargle for catarrh. Tea made from the leaf can be helpful for coughs, vomiting, stomach ache and inflammation of the small intestine.

If you cannot get hold of bilberries, try its North American relative, the blueberry, which also contains high levels of antioxidants.

Blackberry

Predominantly alkali-forming, blackberries are good for the pancreas and liver. Diarrhoea, enteritis, appendicitis, leucorrhoea and catarrh are some of the disorders to which blackberry – usually in tea form – has been applied.

Blackcurrant

High Vitamin C content and the antioxidant anthocyanin in the skins of blackcurrants gives them their anti-bacterial and anti-inflammatory qualities. The juice from the berries can be used for whooping cough in children, as can tea made from the leaves. Blackcurrant tea will also help gout, rheumatism, arterio-sclerosis and throat ailments. Blackcurrant can also help alleviate kidney problems and colicky pains.

Blueberry – see under Bilberry

Brazil nuts

Rich in calcium, Vitamin E and especially in selenium, an antioxidant linked to lowering rates of cancer and heart disease.

Broccoli – see under Cruciferous vegetables

Brussels sprouts – see under Cruciferous vegetables

Buckwheat

This gluten-free seed of a member of the rhubarb family is most commonly used as a substitute for wheat in pasta products and noodles; it can be cooked like rice. Buckwheat is a good source of the flavonoid rutin, which strengthens the walls of the blood vessels, including the tiny capillary vessels, and is thus appropriate as a food in cases of hardening of the arteries and high blood pressure.

Cabbage – see under Cruciferous vegetables

Carrot

High levels of beta-carotene (Vitamin A) and of Vitamins C and E are part of the reason for the all-round health benefits carrots confer on those who eat them regularly. Eyes, skin, liver, lungs, circulation, digestion, and the immune system are all assisted by carrots (eaten raw), as are tardy menstruation, incomplete urination and worms. Made into a soup, carrot soothes diarrhoea, gastro-enteritis and stomach and digestive problems. If possible, always buy organic carrots (see Root vegetables).

Celeriac and celery

The many curative properties of celery are to be found in the root (celeriac), leaves and, especially, the seed, which is available as a tea. It acts on the kidneys as a diuretic, stimulating the excretion of urine, and its anti-inflammatory properties are helpful in cases of rheumatism and arthritis. Celery contains similar anti-ulcer compounds to those found in cabbage. It is also richly endowed with that calming mineral, calcium. The cleansing effect of celery is beneficial for the skin. Celery salt is a good alternative to ordinary salt.

Warning: Use in moderation during pregnancy or if blood pressure is high and not at all if acute kidney problems are present.

Cherry – see under Stone fruit

Chicken

Like game birds, chicken (and turkey) contain less saturated fat than red meat. Organic chickens contain even less of this inflammation-inducing acid, thanks to a natural diet, exercise and the absence of antibiotics and growth promoters. Iron, zinc and the B-complex vitamins are among the nutritional benefits provided by chicken. For centuries it has had a reputation as a restorative in cases of respiratory infection. Certainly its digestibility makes it a valued food for convalescents or those whose digestive system is below par. See page 50 for my recipe for chicken stock.

Chicory

This powerful detoxifier has a cleansing effect on the liver, kidneys and urinary system. It can also be used for stimulating the appetite and digestion, cases of gastritis and jaundice, and problems with the spleen, intestinal catarrh and gallstones. Available in tea form.

Endive is a member of the chicory family and easier to digest than other salad leaves, such as lettuce.

Chilli pepper

The compound that puts the bite into chillies – capsaicin – is also responsible for many of its health-giving properties. These include boosting the immune system, reducing inflammation, alleviating congestion and encouraging expectoration. Evidence also exists to suggest that chillies lower harmful cholesterol, protect against blood clots and prevent stomach ulcers. Experiment carefully with this food as its action may irritate the sensitive gut.

Coffee

The caffeine in coffee has given it a bad reputation as a robber of many important minerals, such as calcium. Some people are adversely affected by it and in them it may trigger headaches or anxiety. Both decaffeinated and ordinary coffee stimulate the secretion of stomach acid, so it is not recommended for those with sensitive stomachs or who are prone to heartburn. Although coffee acts as a laxative in many people, in others it can contribute to constipation, as can tea. The reasons for this constipating effect may be that the nerves in the colon get used to the stimulus of the caffeine and after a while fail to activate the muscles involved in peristalsis, or perhaps that the caffeine draws much needed fluid out of the gut where the stool becomes hard and difficult to shift.

There are coffee substitutes – for example, barley cup and chicory. Go to your local health food store and experiment with what is on offer. Be aware, though, that some people whose systems are fermenting very badly may be sensitive to the starches used in coffee substitutes.

Cous-cous – see under Wheat

Cranberry

With a high Vitamin C content as well as useful amounts of Vitamin A, iron and potassium, cranberry is the most alkali-forming of all the berry fruits. The berries can be eaten whole or made into a juice and used in the treatment of kidney stones, disorders affecting the urinary tract, and diarrhoea (by reducing bodily secretions or discharges). As well as being an appetite stimulant, cranberries are also said to contain anti-cancer and anti-heart-disease properties. An infusion of cranberry leaves can be used to cleanse the bowels.

When you are buying cranberry juice, check the sugar content – many brands sold in supermarkets contain more sugar than cranberries.

Cress *(common garden cress, watercress)*

Cress contains a penicillin-like substance which is helpful in balancing bacteria in the mouth and gut. All cresses contain iodine, which helps regulate the thyroid. It is an appropriate food for kidney complaints (preventing the formation of stones) and is recommended for skin problems. See also under Watercress.

Cruciferous vegetables

This family, which includes cauliflower, swede and turnip as well as those mentioned below, is notable for the protection it gives against cancer, especially of the bladder, breast, colon, throat and prostate. Rich in Vitamins A and C, folic acid, calcium, phosphorus, magnesium and iron, these vegetables contain beta-carotene (a well-documented inhibitor of the growth of cancer cells) in addition to other chemical compounds which check the formation of harmful free radicals. Through these agents the crucifers help support the immune system.

Broccoli – high iron content makes it especially appropriate for those suffering from anaemia, fatigue and stress (emotional or physical).

Brussels sprouts – excessively acid-forming, so eat small amounts and be very wary if you suffer from gout, rheumatism, arthritis or have kidney problems.

Cabbage – contains substances similar to those generated by the mucous membrane of the gut, which make it particularly effective in the treatment of ulcers. The sulphur compounds in cabbage confirm its reputation as a beneficial aid in cases of respiratory infection.

Kale – contains particularly high concentrations of the antioxidant lutein, which is known to protect against blindness as a result of macular degeneration, and of beta-carotene.

Radish – good at stimulating the release of bile, reducing flatulence and soothing diarrhoea, but should be eaten in moderation to avoid irritating the liver, kidneys and gall bladder. Do not use if the stomach or intestines are inflamed.

Cucumber

Cucumbers that are well ripe – indicated by a slight yellowing of the skin – are the most potent for therapeutic purposes. Cucumber has many uses: for heart and kidney problems where there is an inability to eliminate water from the body, kidney and bladder stones, constipation and skin. The juice may be applied externally to inflammations.

Currant – see under Blackcurrant and Redcurrant

Dandelion

This plant has high levels of Vitamins A and C and chlorophyll. It is also a potent source of iron. The young leaves can be used as a salad vegetable, tossed in oil; if you pick them wild, ensure that you wash them thoroughly to eliminate pesticide residues. The Chinese use juice extracted from the plant to treat all kinds of bodily infections, from the lungs to the bladder. Dandelion aids the liver, promoting the formation of bile and removing excess cholesterol and urea. It can also be used to cleanse the body internally and alleviate allied constipation, dyspepsia, and insomnia. Also available as a tea and as a substitute for coffee.

Date

Rich in Vitamin A and easy on the digestion, dates provide a natural source of fructose and gentle stimulation for the bowels. Eat them in moderation, otherwise they will give you wind.

Egg

Although a good source of protein, eggs are not easily digested by all people (especially the whites) and can tax the liver, particularly when they are hard-boiled or eaten with bread. They are most readily tolerated lightly boiled or made into a non-leathery omelette and served with vegetables. Ensure that the eggs you buy are organic to reduce your exposure to salmonella.

Endive – see under Chicory

Fig

Like dates, this mildly laxative fruit has been valued as a food since antiquity. Packed with iron, potassium and calcium, figs are very sustaining, alkali-forming and they contain an enzyme which aids digestion. If dried figs are to be used as a gentle laxative, soak them first. Figs can also be used to soothe irritated mucous membrane; boil them gently in water for a few minutes, allow to steep for a few minutes more, strain and then use.

Fish

All seafood contains Omega-3 fatty acids, but the most potent source of these beneficial fats is fatty fish, such as anchovies, herring, mackerel, fresh salmon, sardines and tuna. These acids protect against heart disease (by lowering levels of cholesterol and triglycerides) and are beneficial for arthritis and bad skin. However, heat destroys Omega-3, and only when fish are eaten raw do their benefits pass intact to the consumer. Baking or poaching fish destroys less of the potency of the fatty acids than frying or grilling. Cooked fatty fish, though, are beneficial for another reason – their digestibility, which the oil facilitates.

Avoid processed fish.

Flax (linseed)

Rich in Omega-3 (alpha-linoleic acid), flax cleanses the arteries, strengthens the immune system, regulates bowel function, lubricates the colon and nourishes the spleen and pancreas. Flax is an abundant source of a group of phyto-chemicals called lignans, which are anti-inflammatory, can lower cholesterol levels, normalise oestrogen levels and can help to regulate blood sugar. The oil from flax is effective in eliminating gall stones.

Flax seeds oxidise very quickly, so it is important to buy them fresh and not already ground or cracked. You can grind the seeds yourself in a coffee grinder before adding them to your food. The seeds are often used as a remedy for constipation. Mixed with water, they swell inside the gut, creating bulk which encourages elimination. Although effective, this remedy is not particularly pleasant as the seeds become gelatinous once they are immersed in water. A way of disguising their consistency is to mix them with a little fruit juice and then add them to a small portion of stewed fruit.

Game birds (grouse, guinea fowl, partridge, pheasant)

For carnivores, these are a healthier alternative to factory-farmed meat, because of their more active – albeit brief – lifestyle and consequently significantly lower content of saturated fat. The arachidonic acid in saturated fat encourages inflammation and blood clotting.

Garlic

There seems to be very little this close relation of the onion is not good for: stimulating digestion, relieving wind, boosting immunity, lifting depression, fighting intestinal infections, regulating actions of the liver and gall bladder, preventing cancer, lowering blood pressure, calming diarrhoea. Cooking garlic, while not destroying all of its health benefits, has an adverse effect on its anti-fungal cleansing, healing properties.

Ginger

This has a multitude of uses, stemming from its cleansing, anti-inflammatory properties: promoting appetite and digestion, encouraging menstruation, alleviating flatulence, colds, sore throat, protecting against arthritis, rheumatism and cancer. The root can be eaten raw, cooked or taken as a tea, infusion or tincture.

Grape *(red)*

Red grapes are high in the antioxidant quercetin and a substance found in their skins is shown to inhibit the formation of blood clots and promote high-density lipoprotein cholesterol, which destroys the type of cholesterol (low-density lipoprotein) that clogs arteries. The cleansing, nutritive properties of grapes make them especially suitable for mono-fasting. Those who suffer from constipation, or who have a badly fermenting gut, should chew the skin and pips thoroughly.

Grapefruit

Contains high levels of Vitamin C, potassium, bioflavonoids and pectin. In addition to being anti-inflammatory and helping the action of Vitamin C, bioflavonoids assist the circulation by strengthening the blood vessels. Pectin is similarly beneficial to those suffering from circulatory disorders, and also helpful to the digestion. Both pectin and bioflavonoids are found in the pith and membranous parts of the fruit.

Greens *(including chard and spinach)*

These are rich sources of folic acid, Vitamins A and C, the minerals calcium and potassium, as well as iron, and the antioxidant lutein, which gives protection against macular degeneration. Spinach is a potent source of antioxidants and compounds that inhibit cancer. However, it is high in oxalic acid – as is chard – and large quantities should not be eaten by people with kidney disorders. Spinach is best eaten raw as cooking destroys many of its nutrients.

Guava

This native to South America is a wonderful source of Vitamin C and also contains high levels of potassium and the fibre pectin. Only a small amount added to a dish will give an exquisite exotic flavour.

Honey

Honey is produced by mixing the nectar from flowers with bee enzymes. The result contains 35 per cent protein, half of all the amino acids and many vital nutrients, such as B-complex vitamins and Vitamins C, D and E. Evidence suggests that honey has strong antibiotic and sedative properties and that it increases the medicinal effect of natural remedies taken for respiratory disorders. When buying honey, try to choose a brand which has not been filtered, heated or otherwise processed. People with low blood sugar should use honey sparingly, because of its relatively high gluco-chemical response.

Kale – see under Cruciferous vegetables

Kiwifruit

High in Vitamins C and E, and potassium, kiwifruit provides all-round health benefits. The Maoris scrub off the hairs and eat the whole fruit, including the skin, which is high in pectin and thus excellent for constipation.

Leek

Leeks have similar, though not as strong, therapeutic properties as those other members of the Allium family, onion and garlic. They are commonly used for stimulating the appetite and relieving respiratory congestion. Because of their high concentrations of potassium, they are particularly appropriate for arthritis and gout sufferers.

Lemon

Containing twice as much Vitamin C as an orange, the lemon has been used to fight infections since time immemorial. The bioflavonoids in lemons help the action of Vitamin C, strengthen the arteries and are anti-inflammatory. As well as being a cleanser, and so good for the joints and respiratory system and for fighting off colds, the lemon is alkali-forming and a great aid to digestion, calming the stomach, expelling wind, and protecting the lining of the gut. That said, if the gut lining is already in bad repair, lemons will point up the problem rather than help it, unless they are mixed in with other food and chewed thoroughly to offset their natural sharpness.

Lentils – see under Pulses

Lettuce

This salad vegetable is a useful source of Vitamin E and so is helpful in promoting the health of the endocrine glands and thus the body's metabolism. In folk medicine lettuce has a place as a cure for insomnia. Leaves must be used when they are fresh if the plant's beneficial effects are not to be lost. However, if you are badly fementing, lettuce may trigger wind unless it is chewed to perfection.

Meat

Beef, lamb and pork contain saturated fat and within this is found a substance called arachidonic acid, which encourages inflammation and blood clotting. The antibiotics and other chemicals which are in the feed of animals raised non-organically contribute to the promotion of acidity in the body. See entries for Chicken and Game birds.

Melon

All types of melon gently stimulate the kidneys and are mildly laxative. Tea made from watermelon is a natural remedy for kidney and bladder disorders. Melons with orange flesh contain the Vitamin A precursor, beta-carotene.

If you find melon wind-forming, try squeezing a few drops of lemon or lime juice on it – this may help.

Milk

Although nutritious, cow's milk has many more problems than benefits attaching to its consumption, largely because its protein is so hard for us humans – especially children, but also adults – to digest. It should certainly be avoided by those with sensitive stomachs or ulcers, as it has been found to stimulate the production of gastric acid and retard the healing of ulcers. The calcium in milk can also be very constipating for some individuals. Goat's and ewe's milk are better alternatives to cow's milk, being easier to digest and nutritionally richer.

However, one by-product of cow's milk should not be dismissed – whey (see page 142).

Millet

A staple in the Far East, Middle East and North Africa, millet is that rare food, an alkali-forming grain which is a complete protein, containing the eight essential amino acids. It also contains B vitamins, iron, and is rich in silicon, a cleansing, healing mineral salt. A valuable nutrient for the organs which convert our food into a usable form, millet may be used like rice and as an alternative to potatoes. Sprouted millet is even more nutritious.

A near relation of millet is sorghum, which has a slightly higher protein content.

Missing Link

Devised by Udo Erasmus, the man behind Udo's Ultimate Oil Blend, this is a top-grade supplement which supplies all the body's nutritional requirements solely from whole foods and food concentrates. The formula contains alfalfa, apple, blackstrap molasses, broccoli powder, carrot, cherry powder, flax seed, garlic, ginger root, hesperidin, kelp, liquorice root, nettle, parsley, rice bran, rosemary, sage, sesame seed, sprouted green barley, spirulina (blue/green algae), sunflower seed, vanilla bean, nutritional yeast and yucca.

Mushrooms

The common button mushroom provides no known health benefits – other than if you love its taste! The most beneficial varieties are Asian, specifically shiitake and maitake, both of which are valued for their ability to stimulate the immune system, fight viral conditions and reduce tumours and blood pressure. In addition, shiitake, maitake and oyster mushrooms are said to lower levels of harmful cholesterol.

Oats

These are very high in calcium, potassium and magnesium and provide useful amounts of iron, phosphorous, zinc, Vitamin E, and the B-complex vitamins (including pantothenic acid). Oats are a wonderful food: nutritious and yet easily digested, and soothing to the digestive tract and on the nerves. In addition to containing antioxidants which help neutralise free radical activity, oats are high in soluble fibre. This type of fibre increases the viscosity of the contents of the gut, which slows the rate at which the enzymes break down the starch, eliciting a lower glucose response than wheat, thus keeping the blood sugar even for longer. This ability to help the body process sugar correctly makes it an especially appropriate food for diabetics. Oatbran, which contains the whole goodness of the grain, is beneficial for everybody, although eaten raw it can be wind-forming. Studies have shown it to be effective in removing bile acids before they can convert into harmful cholesterol.

Jumbo oats, the largest oats available, are made from the whole grain and form the basis of muesli. Porridge is made from coarse oatmeal, although I prefer to use oatbran for this purpose (see page 49) because it has a longer gluco-chemical response.

Oil – see also Berber Argan Oil on page 144

The importance of oil to the process of digestion was confirmed by the German authorities during the Second World War. In one of the innumerable experiments undertaken by them in the concentration camps, they proved that people who were starved and then fed solid proteins would only survive if oil was given with the food. Putting oil on food sends a message to the gall bladder to secrete bile to assist the digestive process. Olive oil is particularly kind to the digestion and when drizzled over starches, such as rice, will slow the rate at which the carbohydrates enter the bloodstream.

Olive oil is a mono-unsaturated fat well endowed with Vitamin E, the most powerful antioxidant and protector against peroxides (free radicals), which can cause cell damage. Regular consumption of olive oil protects against heart disease by increasing the quantity of high-density lipoproteins, or HDLs, in the blood. HDLs remove unhealthy cholesterol or low-density lipoproteins (LDLs) from the bloodstream. In addition to being more digestible than other oils, olive oil increases the secretion of bile, soothes the mucous membranes, promotes intestinal peristalsis, thus easing constipation, and enhances the function of the liver by raising the metabolic rate.

Unrefined virgin olive oil is the best all-purpose oil available, and is as good for cooking as it is for dressing foods. Unlike many other popular oils – safflower, sesame, sunflower, walnut, for example – heat does not change the chemical balance, making it toxic; coconut oil is similarly neutral and thus suitable to cook with. Most of these popular cooking oils are already oxidised when they are bought by the consumer, because of the way they have been processed and subsequently stored. See entry for Flax.

Onion

In addition to being a source of folic acid, calcium, iron, selenium, zinc and vitamins A, C and E, the onion is an outstanding repository of the bioflavonoid quercetin. This substance has powerful anti-cancer (especially of the stomach), anti-inflammatory, anti-viral, anti-clotting and anti-bacterial properties. However, it is only found in shallots and yellow and red onions; it is not present in white onions. The onion has been used to alleviate genito-urinary infections, arthritis, rheumatism, gout, hoarseness and coughs, anaemia, catarrh, cleansing the gastro-intestinal tract, expelling wind, and lowering blood pressure and the levels of harmful cholesterol.

The members of the onion family (including garlic), although good for us in so many ways, can be very wind-forming if the digestion is badly out of balance. Test yourself to discover whether your digestion is strong enough to take them. If it is not, leave them alone for a while and come back to them later.

Orange

This contains high levels of the known inhibitors of cancer, including the antioxidants Vitamin C, beta-carotene, hesperidin (an anti-inflammatory), limonene, and, in the pith and membranes separating the segments, bioflavonoids (Vitamin P), which perform a number of health-promoting functions, such as enhancing the absorption of Vitamin C, relieving pain, stimulating bile production and the circulation and lowering the levels of harmful cholesterol. Oranges – either whole or in juice form – are not advisable for those in whom the gut lining is in poor shape or for arthritis sufferers. Although alkali-forming, they irritate the lining and show up any digestive weakness. Oranges or orange juice tend to be stimulating so it is advisable not to give them to hyper-active children. Healthy children, however, should not experience any problem with them.

Papaya

The effectiveness of papaya as a digestive aid is due to the enzyme papain (similar in its effects to the stomach acid pepsin) which it contains. It is particularly effective in breaking down protein, including intestinal worms.

Parsnip

Rich in calcium, it contains six types of anti-cancer agent as well as Vitamins C and E. Parsnip is also a source of fibre.

Pasta

Semolina or cracked wheat forms the basis of pasta. The best wheat is the durum variety which has a very hard grain. Durum and other hard wheats provoke a lower glucose response than wheat flour, and this response may be reduced still further by ensuring that you cook it 'al dente' and not until it becomes soggy. Whole-wheat pasta is a better source of fibre and the B vitamin thiamine than white pasta. Alternatives to wheat pasta or gluten-free varieties are buckwheat and rice pasta.

Pea

The common garden pea is a good source of Vitamin C and thiamine (B_1), although the blanching that accompanies the processing of frozen peas destroys some of their benefits. The older the pea the more of its natural sugar is converted to starch.

Peach – see under Stone fruit

Pear

Contains the soluble fibre pectin, as well as potassium and Vitamin C. Generally easily digested when ripe.

Pepper

Sweet red and yellow peppers are more nutritious than their younger, green selves, containing beta-carotene – which the body converts into Vitamin A as necessary – and larger amounts of Vitamin C. All peppers contain bioflavonoids or Vitamin P. Green peppers contain a toxin called sotanine to which some people, especially arthritis sufferers, are very sensitive, and in them causes pain and discomfort. See also under Chilli pepper.

Pineapple

An excellent source of Vitamins A and C, folic acid, calcium and potassium. Pineapple also contains manganese, which is needed to make collagen, the protein found in skin, cartilage, ligaments and bone. Another potent constituent of pineapple is the anti-inflammatory enzyme bromelain, which also aids digestion.

Plum – see under Stone fruit

Potato

This staple is probably on most people's list of favourite, healthy foods. Potatoes are not good for everyone, however, particularly the constipated, because the starch in them is very binding. If this is your problem, avoid them or eat them in moderation and ensure that you always bake them, unpeeled, so that the fibre in the skin offsets some of the effect of the starch, and chew them very thoroughly. A tea made from potato peelings is used in many countries as a remedy for high blood pressure. Always remove the sprouts which sometimes appear on potatoes, because these contain a poisonous substance called solanin. White potatoes also contain a toxin called sotanine which interferes with the enzymes in the muscles and causes pain in arthritic people. See also under Sweet potato.

Prune

In their dried form, plums contain useful amounts of potassium and iron, in addition to fibre, sorbitol (a natural sugar) and natural aspirin; they are also easier on the digestion and stomach lining (see entry for Stone fruit). Used wisely (i.e. in moderation), prunes are an excellent laxative, as is the Japanese pickled Umeboshi plum. Do not eat pounds at one go in the mistaken belief that they will provide an instant cure. Eat a few, soaked or cooked.

Pulses (dried beans and peas, lentils)

These provide a non-animal source of protein, and contain minerals (such as iron), fibre, and a range of B-complex vitamins. Pulses lower harmful cholesterol and help to balance blood sugar levels. Many people find them hard to digest quietly, so they need to be prepared carefully. Soak them overnight, rinse them and do not cook them until they begin to sprout. In this state they are much more alkali-forming, more nutritious, and far easier to digest.

Note: The high levels of purines in lentils make them an unsuitable food for gout sufferers.

Pumpkin

Full of beta-carotene, which the body breaks down into Vitamin A, pumpkin protects against cancer and diseases of the heart and respiratory system. Pumpkin seeds supply a range of vitamins and minerals. Correctly processed, oil from the seed retains large amounts of chlorophyll, the 'green blood' of all plant life (see page 141). Use on all kinds of salads, vegetables, pasta and rice dishes, but do not cook with it, as heat destroys its benefits.

Quinoa

Similar to millet but tastier, this high-protein easy-to-digest grain is also a rich source of iron, phosphorus, the B vitamins and Vitamin E. Particularly beneficial for those with weak kidneys. When sprouted, quinoa provides more convertible protein than meat.

Radish – see under Cruciferous vegetables

Raisin

Rich in calcium and a wonderful natural sweetener for muesli or porridge.

Raspberry

High in natural aspirin, and with anti-viral and anti-cancer properties, raspberries are like most other berries alkali-forming, and thus good for the liver and pancreas. Tea made from raspberry leaves soothes diarrhoea.

Redcurrant

The seeds of the berries provide bulk to assist the passage of waste through the bowel. Both the berries and their juice stimulate the digestion and are soothing for an upset stomach. The juice is also helpful as a gargle for a sore throat.

Rhubarb

Despite being full of various vitamins and minerals, rhubarb is a problematic food because it is high in oxalates and thus very acid-forming. It also tends to rob the body of magnesium. If you suffer with arthritis, rheumatism, kidney problems or gout, rhubarb is best avoided completely.

Rice *(whole grain, unpolished)*

Brown rice is one of nature's great healers and I cannot think of any person or condition that it cannot benefit. It is both calming and nutritious, a perfectly balanced whole food. Many people who live outside the areas in which this food has been a staple for centuries now eat rice. Unfortunately most of them do not eat real rice but processed, white rice which is inferior both in flavour and in the health benefits it confers. Brown rice, for example, contains almost ten times more minerals than white rice. The outer cellulose husk, bran and germ are removed during the processing which occurs to produce white rice. What is left may fill the belly but it has been virtually stripped of its B vitamins (especially thiamine), Vitamin E, calcium and phosphorus. Rice provides a good example of how de-naturing a food causes an imbalance. White rice has a constipating effect, purely because of the removal of the bran which in the original unadulterated grain neutralises the binding effect of the starch.

Root vegetables *(carrot, potato, swede, turnip)*

All root vegetables absorb more completely the agents used in their cultivation, both good and bad, so always try to buy organic, because they will contain no residues of chemical pesticides and fertilisers while retaining the trace elements which make them such a valuable food.

Rye

Those who find the gluten in wheat-based foods difficult to digest should try rye, whose gluten content is comparatively low. The whole-rye grain is a valuable source of the B vitamins (especially niacin and riboflavin), potassium and magnesium.

Salt

Ordinary cooking salt, and iodised or fluorinated salt should be avoided for internal use. Sea salt and herbal salt (celery, for example) are much better for us because they contain trace elements which benefit the endocrine glands.

Sesame

The tiny sesame seed contains significant amounts of Omega-9 (oleic acid), Omega-6 (linoleic acid) and selenium. The seeds are widely available and may be eaten as between-meal snacks or sprinkled on salads. Soak them until they swell first to make them easier to digest. See also Oil entry.

Soya

Products made from soya beans, such as tofu, miso and soya milk, are complete proteins, containing all the essential amino acids as well as other nutrients, such as Vitamins A and C and several B vitamins. Soya beans contain a plant hormone, genistein, which helps fight breast, ovarian and prostate cancer. Soya beans help reduce levels of harmful low-density lipoprotein cholesterol and, because they boost oestrogen levels, have a moderating effect on menopausal hot flushes.

Stone fruit *(apricot, cherry, peach, plum)*

Although rich in Vitamins C and E, stone fruit are not suitable for all digestions and should be eaten with great care by those who have problems with their liver or pancreas or who are delicate, either through constitution or a temporary bout of sickness. Even if you are used to eating raw foods and your system accepts them, never eat them on an empty stomach because the hydrocyanic acid in them may upset the intestinal mucous membranes. Stone fruit is more digestible when dried.

Strawberry

Like all other berries, strawberries contain many compounds that are good for health, such as iron. They have a long history of use in medicine, for alleviating gout, reducing blood pressure, and cleansing the gut. Many people are allergic to this fruit, however, possibly because of the chemical fertilisers used in its cultivation, and in some it can adversely affect the kidneys.

Sugar

Refined cane sugar has the effect of increasing acidity, robbing the body of calcium and reducing the effectiveness of our immune system. These negatives largely result from the fact that when it is ingested it goes straight into the bloodstream via the stomach lining. Cane syrup behaves similarly to refined cane sugar and for this reason compares unfavourably with maple syrup or rice syrup. People with low blood sugar are particularly badly affected by sugary foods, which prompt the release of insulin to neutralise the surge in blood sugar. The normal person can usually eat sugar without their glucose levels swinging. Sugar from fruit behaves quite differently, going directly to the liver where much of it is converted slowly to glucose. A wholesome fruit-derived alternative to refined cane sugar is now widely available in the form of fructose.

Also better than refined cane sugar or artificial sweeteners is honey, which retains its trace elements and is also alkali-forming; molasses, too, is preferable, although its heavy flavour demands that it is used sparingly.

Sunflower

A rich source of the essential fatty acid Omega-6 (linoleic acid). The seeds can be eaten whole or ground and then sprinkled on salads. Soak them until they swell first to make them easier to digest. See also Oil entry.

Swede – see under Cruciferous vegetables

Sweet potato

A good source of Vitamins A, B_6, C and E, of fibre and folic acid, and especially of carotenoids, antioxidants which protect us against heart disease, strokes and cancer. Sweet potatoes have a lower glucose response than ordinary potatoes.

Tea

Despite its caffeine content, tea has medicinal benefits, thanks to its chemical compounds which protect the arteries against clots and deposits of harmful cholesterol. The antioxidant, anti-bacterial agents found in tea are called catechins. Asian green tea (the virgin leaves, before they are baked, fermented and labelled black tea) contains far higher levels of these than does black tea and is credited with discouraging the formation of ulcers and a variety of cancers. Rooibos or Redbush tea, which is made from a plant that is native to South Africa (*Aspalathus linearis*), is caffeine-free and contains less than half the tannin found in ordinary tea.

Tomato

In addition to containing useful quantities of Vitamins A, C and E, and of folic acid, biotin, iron, calcium, magnesium and zinc, tomatoes are the primary dietary source of lycopene, a particularly potent antioxidant and inhibitor of free radicals. However, tomatoes are among the foods I ask some of my patients to eliminate from their diet in the beginning, until the gut lining has healed and the fermentation is correct. Some people, especially arthritis sufferers, are sensitive to a toxin in tomatoes called sotanine, which is present in all the so-called nightshade vegetables; aubergines, green peppers and white potatoes are also in this group.

Turnip – see under Cruciferous vegetables

Walnut

Containing high levels of Omega-6 (51 per cent) and considerably less Omega-3 (5 per cent) as well as an antioxidant called ellagic acid, walnuts stimulate the liver and influence the bowels. They are often recommended as a good food for constipation sufferers. However, the ellagic acid can irritate the stomach lining; for this reason some cultures soak the nuts in salt water to lessen its effects.

Water

The average person requires a minimum of 1.8 litres (3 pints) every day to maintain good health; the constipated should drink double this amount, as should those who are on a detoxifiying regime. The gut absorbs water to help in the removal of waste. Without sufficient water, waste stays in the system longer and deposits may remain clinging resolutely to the walls of the digestive tract to create a disturbance of one sort or another.

So, what sort of water should you drink: tap, Natural Mineral Water, natural water, table water, spring water, distilled? There are clear differences between these types. All of them, apart from Natural Mineral Water, may have been chemically cleaned or processed. Despite the rigorous 'cleaning' that goes into making tap water potable, certain hormones and non-biodegradable substances remain in it, and the fact that so many chemicals are involved in the cleaning process destroys any idea of it being a 'natural' drink.

That word 'natural' is bandied about quite freely in descriptions of the various types of water, so if you are concerned about the provenance of the water you drink, be vigilant about what you buy. As the law stands at the time of writing, it is perfectly legal for so-called natural or table waters to be drawn from an underground source of indeterminate quality and consistency and then purified or treated to make them safe to drink. Indeed so-called table water can be no more than filtered tap water. Spring water is a slightly different matter. New regulations mean that it must come from, and be bottled at, a single, identified source. However, it need not be consistent in content and may be treated to change its composition.

Distilled water is virtually H_2O which has been evaporated and condensed. By definition it has been engineered and is often described as 'dead' water, containing none of the trace elements found in Natural Mineral Water. Be very careful with distilled or purified water because its molecular structure, while facilitating the removal of heavy toxins from the body in treatments geared to those with severe, degenerative illnesses, can be detrimental to the healthy by leaching essential minerals out of normal cells.

Flavoured waters are no substitute for Natural Mineral Water, either. In the main these are clear, sweetened soft drinks and few of them use Natural Mineral Water as their base. Most of them are very high in calories and contain artificial rather than real ingredients.

Natural Mineral Water must come from an identified and protected source, must be of known and consistent quality and must be naturally wholesome without treatment. Natural Mineral Water status is granted only to waters which are demonstrated to be free from pollution and to have a characteristic stable composition. The purest water for drinking is 'Natural Mineral Water', so look for this complete phrase when choosing bottled water and do not be seduced by labels which show only a plausible brand name and a picture of rushing torrents. However, if you cannot get nor afford Natural Mineral Water, any kind of water is better than too little, so do not give up on it altogether. Your gut needs it.

Note: People with high blood pressure who wish to buy Natural Mineral Water should look for a brand which has a very low sodium content (under 10 mg per litre [1³/4 pt]). It is also advisable to give this type to infants and young children. All water given to babies under 6 months should always be boiled and cooled first.

Watercress

An excellent source of folic acid, Vitamins A, C and E and the minerals calcium, magnesium, potassium, iron and of a modest amount of iodine, it also contains the antioxidant lutein (which helps prevent macular degeneration). Watercress helps regulate the endocrine glands, including the thyroid, lower blood pressure, and keep the arteries healthy. Catarrh, anaemia, gout, tuberculosis and mild indigestion are helped by watercress. Use fresh. Do not eat daily because of risk of kidney damage, and, if you are pregnant, eat it in moderation. See also under Cress.

Wheat

The protein gluten is what makes wheat products so indigestible for many people. The degree to which it has been processed also has an effect on how our bodies deal with it. Wheat that has been milled into fine flour is broken down quickly by the starch-digesting enzymes in the gut, eliciting a fast glucose response.

Wholemeal flour is no different from white flour in this respect. If wheat can be tolerated, it is best for dietary and health purposes to use the forms that have not been finely ground. With bread, for example, choose the kind which contains large amounts of whole grains, because these, in addition to providing valuable vitamins and minerals, have slower rates of digestion and absorption. Generally with wheat the smaller the particle size the faster is the action of the enzymes and thus the faster and higher the glycaemic response. Sourdough bread – in which the gluten has been fermented out – may provide an acceptable alternative for people who find the gluten in wheat difficult to cope with. People who are completely wheat intolerant should try one of the many gluten-free flours that are available.

Wheat bran is often recommended as a protective against developing colon cancer. However, depending on how the gut is fermenting, it can do more harm than good because it tends to be wind-forming and can irritate – and even inflame – the lining, especially in individuals whose digestive tracts are not in good order, such as those with gastritis or ulcers. Wheat germ contains the nutritional potency of the whole grain and is a valuable source of Vitamin E. Even people in whom the fermentation is not right can usually get away with eating some wheat germ. If it does cause digestive problems, try oat germ or rice germ instead. Invariably, I counsel people to eat oatbran in preference to wheat germ or wheat bran because of its greater benefits (see entry for Oats).

Whole-wheat processed by means of cracking, hulling, parboiling and roasting produces bulgar or burghal wheat. Far from destroying the nutrients, this process – especially the parboiling – actually preserves them, concentrating them in the centre of the grain.

Like bulghar, cous-cous – which is made from coarse-grade semolina, the starchy endosperm of the wheat grain – can be used as a low-glucose response substitute for rice. Because both forms of wheat have been pre-cooked, they are easily digested – and easily cooked too, requiring only to be re-constituted with boiling water and then mixed with onion, parsley and any vegetables of your choice to make a nourishing main meal.

Yoghurt

Natural yoghurt contains Vitamins A, D, the B-complex and, most importantly, *Lactobacillus acidophilus* and other 'friendly' bacteria. The lactic fermentation which plays a role in the making of yoghurt renders the end result more digestible than, say, a glass of fresh cow's milk. However, goat's (especially) and sheep's yoghurt are less mucus-forming and particularly recommended for those who suffer with their sinuses. Artificially sweetened yoghurt should be avoided because sugar feeds 'unfriendly' bacteria.

Herbs

There are simply hundreds of herbs which have beneficial properties – more than 500 are listed by the Greek doctor Dioscorides in his *De Materia Medica*, the first European exposition of the uses and characteristics of medicinal plants, published in the first century AD. Earlier the Sumerians, Egyptians and Chinese had studied herbs and produced accounts of their uses. As with other plants, herbs which are familiar to us purely as culinary aids – such as garlic, caraway, thyme, mint and bay – were used by them as both foods and medicines.

Herbs generally are good for the digestion. Some, like dill, are mild and good for reducing flatulence. Others are stronger tasting and provide additional health benefits. However, if you do not like the taste of, for example, rosemary, there seems little point in using it. There are so many herbs to choose from that if one does not suit your palate an appropriate alternative is sure to be found. As with food generally, there are no hard and fast rules about using herbs. How you like to combine foods and ingredients in a dish is individual to you and your particular taste-buds. I have provided information on each herb's uses in folk medicine. The rest is up to you.

Allspice

Use for: flatulence, indigestion, stimulating appetite, neuralgia, rheumatism.

Amaranth

Use in tea form for: diarrhoea, haemorrhoids, heavy menstruation, stomach ulcers, internal bleeding. May also be used as a skin wash and as a douche for leucorrhoea.

Anise

This herb is often used in imitation of liquorice, which has been attributed with anti-cancer and anti-bacterial properties as well as being helpful in the treatment of ulcers and diarrhoea. Anise does not contain the same properties, although it is beneficial in other respects. Use for: cramps, indigestion, colic (especially in children), nausea, insomnia, low blood pressure, promoting lactation.

Barberry

Use for: mouth or throat irritations and as a wash for strengthening the gums; the ripe berries have a laxative effect. The berries are alkaline-forming and used widely in Iranian cooking; supermarkets which stock Iranian food products are the easiest source. Decoctions of the berries or root can be obtained from herbalists.

Basil

Use for: stimulating the appetite, constipation, stomach cramps, flatulence, enteritis, migraine, whooping cough, promoting lactation.

Bay (laurel)

Use for: stimulating the digestion; a decoction made from the leaves and mixed with honey to make a syrup can be applied to the chest to alleviate colds or chest problems.

Birch

Use in tea form for: (leaf) urinary problems, kidney stones, intestinal worms; (bark) diarrhoea, rheumatism, boils.

Calendula

Use as tincture or infusion for: ulcers, stomach cramps, diarrhoea, gastritis, menstrual problems, fever, abscesses and boils. Also useful as a salve for healing wounds.

Camomile

Use in tea form for: nervous disorders, insomnia, rheumatism, neuralgia, lumbago, reducing inflammation, helping the bowels to move without causing an explosion. Bathing in camomile or using a camomile salve can help haemorrhoids.

Caraway

Use for: stimulating appetite and digestion, flatulence, uterine cramps, catarrh, promoting lactation.

Cardamom

Use for: stimulating appetite and the digestive process, flatulence.

Cayenne (Capsicum)

Use for: stimulating the appetite. Only consume in small quantities, as too much cayenne can cause gastro-enteritis and kidney damage.

Chervil

Use for: stimulating the digestion, arterio-sclerosis, lowering blood pressure, menopause, skin, incomplete urination

Chive

Use for: stimulating appetite and promoting digestion, anaemia.

Clove

Use for: toothache, vomiting (oil of clove). Clove tea will stop nausea.

Coriander

Use seeds for: promoting appetite, expelling wind, stimulating and strengthening the stomach, soothing indigestion.

Dill

Use for: stimulating the appetite, flatulence, insomnia, promoting the flow of milk in nursing mothers. Dill tea is used for upset stomach. Chewing the seeds helps halitosis.

Fennel

Use seeds for: stimulating the appetite, relieving colic, stomach cramps and flatulence, expelling mucus. Fennel oil helps coughs and hoarseness and can be used externally to relieve rheumatic pains.

Fenugreek

Use for: bronchitis, fevers, expelling mucus, aiding recovery from illness, sore throat, balancing the blood sugar, strengthening the digestion. Available in dried and leaf form from Iranian supermarkets. Growing fenugreek from seed (available from health shops) is very easy.

Hawthorn

Use in tea form for: stress, nervous disorders, insomnia.

Horseradish

Use for: rheumatism, gout, bladder infections, colitis, catarrh, coughs, sinus, asthma.

Note: Only fresh horseradish is effective. You can ensure that its volatile oils are retained by grating it into lemon juice. It will keep for about a week in this form.

Juniper

Use berries for: under-production of hydrochloric acid, stimulating the appetite, flatulence, gastro-intestinal infection, inflammation and cramp, eliminating excess water, rheumatic pains. May irritate the kidneys and urinary tract if taken in large doses or used over a long period.

Lavender

Use leaves or oil for: cleansing the intestines, stomach problems, nausea, vomiting, flatulence, migraine, dizziness.

Lemon balm

Use in tea form for: nervous conditions, melancholy, insomnia, cramps, dyspepsia, flatulence, colic and catarrh.

Marjoram, wild *(oregano)*

Use for: calming the stomach, indigestion, headache, nervous disorders, respiratory disorders, abdominal cramps, regulating the menstrual cycle.

Milk thistle

Use in tea form for: stimulating the appetite, soothing indigestion, and aiding the correct functioning of the liver.

Mint *(peppermint)*

Use for: stimulating the digestive processes, heartburn, nausea, stomach cramps, nervous disorders, palpitations, migraine, insomnia. Spearmint (garden mint) helps with urinary problems in addition to those given above.

Mugwort *(Artemisia)*

Use for: stimulating the appetite and digestive processes, regulating menstruation. It is frequently used in combination with other herbs.

Mullein

Use in tea form for: bronchial and chest disorders, digestive problems, inducing sleep.

Mustard *(white and black)*

Use for: stimulating the appetite and digestive processes, bronchitis, constipation. Only use in small amounts, especially the black variety.

Nasturtium

Use in tea form for: respiratory congestion, internal cleanser, promoting the formation of blood cells.

Nettle

Use for: excessive menstrual flow, stimulating the digestion, promoting the flow of milk in nursing mothers, haemorrhoids, diarrhoea.

Nutmeg

Use for: stimulating the appetite and digestive processes. Eat in small quantities only.

Oregano – see Marjoram

Parsley

Use for: expelling wind, kidney problems, strengthening the constitution, easing constipation, disguising the odour of garlic. Also available as a tea, for stimulating the kidneys.

Rosemary

Use for: stimulating the digestion, promoting the production of bile, circulatory problems.

Note: Use in moderation as the ingestion of excessive amounts of rosemary can cause fatal poisoning.

Sage

Use for: night sweats, nervous disorders, diarrhoea, gastritis, respiratory congestion, menstrual problems.

Note: Prolonged and excessive use of sage can give rise to symptoms of poisoning.

Sorrel

Fresh sorrel leaves can be used like spinach as part of a bodily 'spring clean'. Sorrel tea may be helpful as a diuretic in encouraging urination and as a remedy for mouth and throat ulcers.

Note: Excessive consumption of sorrel can result in kidney damage.

Star anise

Use for: stimulating the appetite and promoting digestion, relieving flatulence.

Tarragon

Use for: digestive difficulties, catarrh, stimulating the kidneys, encouraging menstrual flow, insomnia. Available as a tea.

Thyme

Use for: cough, cramps, flatulence, diarrhoea, gastritis, stimulating the appetite.

Note: Excessive consumption can lead to over-activating the thyroid gland.

Valerian

Use in tea form for: nervous disorders, insomnia, fatigue, stomach cramps. Strong doses taken for prolonged periods may produce symptoms of poisoning.

Verbena/ Vervain

Use in tea form for: congestion associated with colds, insomnia, nervous conditions, intestinal worms.

Supplements

It is very easy to be seduced into believing that a capsule or spoonful of some exotic elixir will solve all our health or dietary problems. Popping a pill is always less of a bother than changing how we eat. I view supplements with caution for this very reason, because they can divert us from the more difficult task of addressing the fundamentals of a problem. All the supplements I recommend aid the central aim of building a healthy gut. They help correct individual areas of weakness and, like cogs in a wheel, each of them has a role to play. But – and it is an emphatic but – neither separately nor collectively are they a cure-all. It is wise to understand their virtues, use them appropriately and expect their effectiveness to match your level of commitment to the eating plan.

Acidophilus

The microflora in the gut must be in good shape if the body is to absorb and utilise minerals and vitamins effectively. Probiotics such as Acidophilus facilitate the growth of a healthy intestinal ecosystem.

Only small amounts of the very mildest form of Acidophilus should be taken in the first instance by those whose digestion is poor and whose colon or bowel has been subjected to irritation for a long time. Too strong a dose introduced into a stomach where the lining is already raw will only make the situation worse, probably prompting nausea and sickness as the body tries to eliminate this new irritant. Another group that should take especial care includes those who suffer with asthma or skin problems or have had several courses of antibiotics in quick succession. Going in robustly with Acidophilus and killing off the bad bacteria too quickly may produce an allergic reaction, such as headache. Be prepared to proceed slowly and cautiously.

I use a specially made blend of Acidophilus from Sweden, called Gut Reaction Probion, which I find is less likely to cause problems. I may also suggest that patients use Super-5, a pleasant tasting probiotic containing five specific friendly micro-organisms for the mouth, gums and large and small intestines.

When giving Acidophilus to infants, always use a model that is appropriate for them, and proceed with great care, testing as you go, because the digestive systems of children react much faster than do those of adults.

Cal-M

The principal ingredients of this instant-drink powder are calcium and magnesium which work together to combat free radicals and stress. The heart, nervous system and muscles all benefit from Cal-M. In addition to having a very calming effect on the digestive system, Cal-M makes the body more alkaline and feeds the liver. I find that mixing it into a fibre drink or with a few cooked stewed prunes at night is beneficial and helps people to wake up brighter in the morning.

Digestive enzymes

There are two sources of digestive enzymes: our digestive system and food. The body produces enzymes to break down food into its basic components for absorption, but as we age our ability to man-ufacture them diminishes. Stress, alcohol, smoking and caffeine also deplete our reserves of enzymes. All raw food contains the enzymes required for its digestion. Chewing releases these – except that most of us do not chew our food well enough to activate them and much of the raw food we eat has been grown in poor soil. Cooking and processing foods destroys digestive enzymes too. All-in-all most of us over the age of forty-five have a shortfall.

In most cases I use Udo's Ultimate Digestive Enzyme Blend, a plant-based supplement containing all the enzymes required to digest the full range of food types, especially protein. For patients with extra-sensitive guts I may use Biocare's Digestive Aid.

When using digestive enzymes, people with very sensitive stomachs need to ensure that the gut lining is not irritated. To avoid this, I recommend that, in the beginning, they open the cap-sule and use only about a quarter of its contents, mixing it with a bit of food to test it. With all supplements it is wise always to err on the side of caution and take less than the recommended dose.

Fibre

This is used for softening stools and cleaning the intestines. One of the cheapest fibres is linseed, which should be soaked overnight or cooked with a little oatbran to soften it – if you sprinkle the raw seeds on food and then ingest them they will stick to the gut and give you wind and maybe a great deal of discomfort. Another common fibre, psyllium, although effective, also promotes wind. This is not helpful if someone is already fermenting badly. The fibre I value above all others is FructoOligoSaccharide (F.O.S.), which I call Oligo-fibre. This product feeds the right bacterial flora as well as assisting in establishing and maintaining regular bowel movements. Taking Oligo-fibre in tandem with Acidophilus will speed up the rate at which 'friendly' bacteria re-colonise the gut. Oligo-fibre also tastes pleasant and can be taken with food without drawing attention to itself; it can even be used as a sugar substitute (see page 100), and in this respect is particularly useful for children who are constipated. However, use sparingly in the beginning; otherwise, you may get spectacular wind. Transitibiane can also be useful in some cases.

Whichever fibre you choose to take, always drink plenty of water with it.

L-glutamine

This amino acid is the main fuel of the gut lining and, like the other amino acids, ensures that maximum absorption from food is achieved. L-glutamine in powder form is kinder on very delicate stomachs than capsules, which may cause irritation. This supplement is heat- and acid-sensitive and should not be mixed into foods or beverages which are hot or acid. L-glutamine may also be used as a direct means of feeding the pancreas and liver in those whose bodies are under pressure, as a consequence of stress, illness or over-indulgence in alcohol or rich food.

Slippery elm

The inner bark of the slippery elm plant provides this nutritious, soothing supplement. Powdered slippery elm food is especially valuable in cases where the stomach lining is inflamed and, as a result, most foods are problematic.

Super-foods

There are a number of products available which utilise the qualities of plants that are nutrient dense and, because they are at or near the bottom of the food chain, relatively free from contamination. These 'green energy' super-foods are ideal for people whose energy levels tend to dip between meals, and can easily be mixed into juices, stewed fruit or yoghurt for consumption at work or home. Vitamins and minerals given to the body in the form of natural foods are more readily and completely assimilated than those processed into capsules and tablets.

Udo's Missing Link, which combines a host of whole foods and food concentrates (see page 118), is one super-food product I use a lot. It is especially good for people with low blood sugar who need to feed their bodies between meals. However, it may be too harsh for the guts of those suffering with diarrhoea or who are in the diarrhoea phase of IBS.

There are other products providing similar nutritional benefits which you may like to try:

Freshwater micro-algae such as spirulina and chlorella, for example, are the richest known sources of chlorophyll, which is a great cleanser (of the blood, kidneys, liver and bowel), stimulator of growth and the metabolism, strengthener of the immune system and facilitator of absorption. Sea-water algae include plankton and seaweed (such as kelp) and are rich sources of iodine as well as other minerals and vitamins. Iodine is necessary for the healthy functioning of the thyroid gland and for the body's mental and physical development. It helps to metabolise excess fat and so is a useful supplement for the overweight. An insufficiency of iodine has also been linked to breast cancer. There are also mineral-rich sea vegetables such as dulse, nori and wakame. Irish moss, or carrageen, is another long-valued alga and has been used for centuries to help manage intestinal problems, tuberculosis, bronchitis and coughs.

Land-based super-foods include grasses such as alfalfa, oat and spelt. Barley grass, for example, is an excellent source of calcium, iron, the essential amino acids, Vitamin C, Vitamin B_{12}, and many minerals plus enzymes. It is an anti-inflammatory and nourishes the blood, intestines, gall bladder, pancreas, duodenum, stomach and nerves. The plant aloe vera is an all-round healer of organs and cell tissue, energising the whole body, stimulating digestion, alleviating constipation, reducing inflammation and repairing damaged tissue. (*Note:* Diabetics may develop an intolerance to aloe vera juice.)

Royal jelly has a long reputation as a super-tonic. The jelly consists of the nutritive fluid produced by honey bees to feed queen bees. Royal jelly is the richest natural source of pantothenic acid (B_5), which is essential to the proper functioning of the gastrointestinal tract.

All the aforementioned super-foods are relatively expensive. Much cheaper yet highly effective is old-fashioned brewer's yeast. Despite its unpromising-sounding name, brewer's yeast is packed with vital nutrients and is a complete food. Its high levels of the B-complex vitamins and of iron, zinc, manganese, magnesium, potassium, and the nucleic acid RNA (essential to the proper functioning of the immune system), make it a formidable food for those under stress and in need of a boost. Many people these days shy away from anything containing yeast for fear that it may trigger an allergic reaction. Brewer's yeast, however, is good for most people, with the exception of those who should avoid foods containing purines (i.e. people with gout or joint problems).

Another factor that has probably told against brewer's yeast is its taste, which many people find off-putting. You will have to work hard to disguise it, but it is worth it, especially if you are on a limited budget. If you decide to try it, be sure to take calcium as well, to balance its phosphorus content. You can either add some powdered calcium before beating it into fruit juice, or beat the yeast directly into goat's milk, which contains sufficient calcium to provide the correct balance.

The most alkali-forming of the super-foods is goat's whey. Whey is the part of the milk (cow's, goat's or sheep's) discarded during cheese making. Far from being a waste by-product, whey contains most of milk's nutritional riches and, most importantly, enzymes. Whey especially benefits those with very poor digestion in whom absorption is a problem and the bacterial flora are unbalanced. A convenient form of whey or lactic acid is Vogel's Molkosan; a tablespoon of this taken in water before a meal will aid the fermentation.

Epilogue

THE FRAILTY PACKAGE

Most people abuse themselves in some way, shape or form every now and again, even those of us who some might think should know better. Life is for living and some of the most pleasurable pursuits automatically seem to exact retribution. At the risk of ruining my credibility, I must state that I think it is no bad thing for someone in my position to be fully human in this respect. I can still fall for that drink or nibble too far and pay the price later in a hangover or upset stomach. This section is a sort of first aid to help you recover more quickly from those occasional bouts of over-indulgence.

The result of eating, smoking or drinking too much is that the body becomes a pit of toxicity. Alcohol and tobacco are natural toxins – and no better for that fact – and you should know by this stage of the book that over-eating creates a state of toxicity in the gut. Over-indulgence is a bit like driving into a cul-de-sac – there is no way out except by the route you came in. In other words, when you stray from the path of nutritional virtue, you have to re-trace your steps and bring the body back into balance by restoring alkalinity.

Picking Yourself Up

The morning after the night before, go back to square one. Start the day with a steaming mug of ginger and lemon (see page 67). Whenever we are feeling the worse for wear, the blood sugar tends to be in a trough. This is particularly the case with low blood sugar people, whose levels even on good days will not raise themselves above knee height without assistance. Mix some 'green energy' food such as Missing Link (see page 118) or the amino acid L-glutamine into a drink mid-morning and afternoon. Before eating, take some whey or lactic acid to encourage alkalinity. The liver is particularly put under pressure when we consume too much alcohol or rich food – puffy eyes are a sign that it is not coping well – and it needs all the help it can get in the form of foods which will not make the system more acid. Often after a binge the body will tell you that it wants starches. Resist the temptation to give in to these cravings, which to the hungover body are what 'cold turkey' is to the drug-abused. You need foods which contain B vitamins – 'green energy' will provide these – and those which will not require it to work hard. Chicken soup (see page 51) for stock is a wonderfully warming, nutritious pick-me-up and would be the wisest choice of 'solids'. Follow this regime for however long it takes you to recover.

Colds require a similar course of action. Use warming and cleansing teas such as cinnamon, liquorice and elderberry flower, in addition to ginger and lemon. Eat lightly, avoiding foods that will raise your glucose levels quickly. Chicken or vegetable soups will be your best option until you feel well enough to tackle more interesting food.

BERBER ARGAN OIL

Argan oil is the product of the Argan Treenut (*Argania spinosa*). It is a tree whose origin goes back 85 million years. It grows in the south west of Morocco and nowhere else in the world. Gudrun is passionate about this oil and uses it for most of her clients. Among its many benefits are:

hair care, to add body and life
stimulates and develops brain functions
aids healthy pregnancy
relieves dry and itchy scalp
skin care for dry skin
helps diminish wrinkles
relieves arthritic pains
used for eczema, acne and other skin conditions
chapped lips
burns

breaking nails
rheumatic pains.

Stated uses in university research publications:
stabilises high cholesterol by increasing the level of good cholesterol
reduces high blood pressure
fights obesity by reducing hunger pangs
helps liver function
neutralizes free radicals
stimulates cellular exchanges and improves intercellular material
acts against the drying and ageing of skin by restoring the hypolipid and by increasing cellular nutritional intake
schottenol, an anti-carcinogen, is found in argan oil
because of its high sterol content it can be substituted for cholesterol in cosmetic products
Methylene-24 cycloartanol assists the body to rid itself of cholesterol through an increased digestion and excretion of stomach acids.

The composition of argan oil makes it ideal for culinary, cosmetic or medicinal use. The nutritional elements in the oil facilitate digestion by increasing the amount of pepsin in digestive fluids. 16 grams (2 tablespoons) of oil assures the body's daily need of linoleic acid. The absence of linolenic acid gives argan a long shelf life. The anti-oxidant action is due to the presence of phenolic elements. The percentage of polyunsaturated fats to that of saturated fats is 1.9 and very close to the 1-1.5 recomended by nutritionalists.

Gudrun has now developed a range of beauty products which are available from her practice and also via her web page.

RESOURCES

The following practitioners are highly recommended by the author. Gudrun Jonsson has been treated by them all and has benefited enormously from their individual talents, helping her to maintain good health. She often refers her patients to them when appropriate.

1) **Ginny Struthers BA BSC. OST.NLP.DIP HYP. Registered Osteopath**

   Ginny practises alongside Gudrun and has been an osteopath and master neuro linguistic programmer for many years. Her work is exceptional and her use of cranial osteopathy very successful within the practice. To make an appointment with Ginny call 020 7486 1711.

2) **Dr Franklin's Panchakarma Institute & Research Centre**, Chowara P.O., Thiruvananthapuram, Kerala, S. India. Pin-695 501. Tel: 0091-471-480870, Fax: 0091-471-482870.

3) **The Natural Mineral Water Information Service** publishes a free booklet, Body Thoughts, about the benefits of drinking water. For a copy send a stamped self-addressed DL envelope to: Natural Mineral Water Information Service, PO BOX 6, Hampton, Middlesex TW12 2HH. For further information from the Natural Mineral Water Information Service visit the website http://www.naturalmineralwater.org

4) **Bodydoctor fitness**

   David Marshall is the fitness expert who I work with and he keeps us all in shape. For information, tel: 020 7586 6222 or visit his website on: www.bodydoctorfitness.com
   Email: david@bodydoctorfitness.com

Gudrun's practice is now offering beauty treatments using her own argan oils and creams. For more information please call 020 7486 1711.

To find out more about Gudrun's London practice or the products she recommends, you can find us on the worldwide website at:
http://www.gudrunjonsson.com
or
gudrunsproducts@legado.co.uk
or telephone us on 020 7486 1711;
or write to us enclosing an s.a.e. at: 2 Napier Road, London W14 8LQ, England.
Note: You can order most of the products mentioned in this book from our website as above or by contacting the practice. Many of the products are also available from H. Lloyd Chemist, tel: 020 7603 4761.

INDEX

acid-alkaline response 4–5, 8, 15, 25, 42
acidic foods 5, 27, 39
acidity 3, 28, 34–5, 41, 42, 66
Acidophilus 25, 40, 47, 96, 138
alcohol 6, 9, 102–3, 139, 143–4
alfalfa 103
algae 141
almonds 103–4
aloe vera 142
amino acids 3, 25, 65, 140
apple 35, 36, 40, 46, 48, 104
apple crumble, spiced 90
apricot 104
artichoke, globe 105
asking for help 13–14
asparagus 84, 105
aubergine 61, 105
avocado 39, 86, 105–6
    recipes 51, 76

bacteria 2–3, 5, 25, 107
    see also microflora
banana 91, 106
barberry 81, 132
barley 106
bedtime snack 97
beer 103
belching 16, 17
beetroot 106–7
beetroot soup with chives 73
beta-carotene 6, 104, 108
bilberry 41, 107
bile 6, 20, 28, 119
binding foods 33
Biocare Digest Aid 41, 47, 139
Biosalt 65
blackberry 107
blackcurrant 107
bloating 12, 25, 97

blood sugar 6, 7, 8, 26
    low 7, 20, 21–3, 29, 34, 38, 40, 45, 67,
        68, 69, 96, 97, 106, 126, 141, 143
bolting food 30
bowel movements 19–20, 97
Bragg's Liquid Aminos 65
bran 39, 130
Brazil nuts 108
bread 26, 42, 44, 96
breakfast cereal 41, 46, 98
brewer's yeast 142
broccoli 33, 87
buckwheat 108
bulgar wheat 130
butter 66

cabbage 33
caffeine 22, 109, 127, 139
Cal-M 37, 65, 97, 139
calcium 6, 109, 139, 142
camomile 47, 133
carbohydrates 22–3, 26, 32, 96
carrots 33, 39, 95, 108
cauliflower/broccoli gratin 87
celeriac/celery 33, 39, 108–9
charcoal 41
cheese 15, 33, 66
chemical additives 6, 103
chermoula dressing 78
chewing 4, 7, 8, 12, 18, 23, 26, 29, 30–1,
        33, 40, 45, 96, 139
chicken 39, 44, 109
    recipes 53, 58, 60, 82, 83
chicken soup 57, 144
chicken stock 50–1, 70
chicory 33, 109
children 11, 94–101, 138, 140
chillies 109
chlorophyll 103, 141

cider vinegar 65
coconut milk 66
coconut recipes 80, 93
coffee 7, 66, 109–10
colds 144
constipation 11, 17, 19–21, 24, 25, 46,
        97, 101
    eating plan 32–7
    recipes 51–6
courgette 39, 61
cous-cous 130
crab and avocado salad 86
cranberry 110
cress 110
cucumber 111
custards 93

dairy products 15, 66, 101
dandelion 112
dates 112
detoxification 2, 6, 25, 109
diarrhoea 20, 24, 25, 141
    eating plan 37–41, 46
digestive system 1–6, 103
dill 41, 59, 76, 134
dressings 76–80
drinks, warm 34, 36, 40, 45, 98

eating habits 13, 30–1, 40
eggs 33, 67, 112
emotional state 12, 45
endive 109
energy 22, 26, 32–3, 37, 45, 141
enteric nervous system 12
enzymes 4, 8, 13, 18, 20, 26, 30, 43, 96,
        103, 139
    supplements 25, 33, 35, 41, 44, 45,
        47, 139
exclusion diets 15
exercise 31

fats 2, 6, 7, 32, 109
fennel 33, 52, 72, 81, 134
fermentation 5–6, 12, 26, 38–9
fermented foods 28
fibre 19, 35, 36, 47, 139–40
figs 112
fish 12, 39, 44, 113
    recipes 52, 59, 86

flatulence, *see* wind
flax, *see* linseed
food allergies 3, 14–15
food combining 26, 96
food preparation 27–9
fructose 71, 100, 126
fruit 27, 67, 96, 99–100, 125
    compote 92
    stewed 40–1, 46, 47, 67, 99

gall bladder 35, 119
game birds 113–14
garlic 114
gastric acids 4–5, 13, 20, 25, 27, 28, 30,
        110
genes 1, 9–10, 14–15, 96
ginger 67, 114
ginger and lemon drink 67, 143
gluten 26, 41, 129–30
glycaemic response 22–3, 26, 28, 69, 130
grain 33, 44
grapefruit 114
grapes 114
grasses 141
green energy foods 36, 46, 141, 143, 144
greens 33, 115
guava 115
gut lining 2–3, 5, 15, 24–7
Gut Reaction Probion 35, 47, 138

hangover pick-me-up 143–4
herb teas 36, 40, 46, 67, 144
herb sauces 57, 69
herbs 27, 28, 65, 67, 131–7
    chewing 35, 47
honey 66, 68, 96, 100, 115, 126
hunger 4, 22, 28, 29–30

ices 91
immune system 7, 12, 43, 103
indigestion 12, 17–18, 20, 40, 106
insulin 7, 23, 126
iodine 141
iron 4, 6, 25
irritated bowel 10, 19, 20–1, 24
    eating plan 41–7

juices 36, 68
junk food 22, 23

kiwi fruit 35, 115
Kuzu (arrowroot) 40, 41, 68

L-glutamine 3, 25, 40, 140, 143
lactic acid 28, 142, 144
lamb recipes 52, 54, 81
leaky gut syndrome 2–3
leeks 116
lemon 5, 28, 40, 46, 60, 116
lemon grass 52, 68, 80
lentils 54, 75, 123
lettuce 116
lime leaves 68
linseed 36, 113, 139–40
liver 6, 8, 28, 48, 103, 139, 140, 144

magnesium 139
main meals 51–63, 81–9
maintenance recipes 24, 72–94
malabsorption 3, 25
mange-tout 39, 58, 95
maple syrup 71, 89, 100
mayonnaise, herb 79
meal times 13
meat 27–8, 33, 39, 116–17
melon 91, 117
metabolic rate 28, 34
microflora 2, 9, 15, 20, 25, 28, 45, 131, 138, 140
mid-morning/-afternoon 34, 45
middle age 30, 43
migraine 103
milk 66, 96–7, 98, 101, 117
millet 117
minerals 4, 10, 29, 141
Missing Link 36, 41, 46, 67, 68, 99, 118, 141, 143
molasses 71, 126
Molkosan 90, 140
mushrooms 118

noodle soup, oriental 74
nutrients 2, 3, 26

oats 69, 96, 118
oils 39, 69, 119
Oligo-fibre 36, 71, 100–1, 140
olive oil 28, 69, 119
    and lemon drink/sauce 35, 46, 47, 48, 59, 69, 77

omelette, herb 57
onions 119–20
oranges 120
over-eating 5, 6, 8, 19, 26, 29, 32, 143

packed lunches 98–9
pancreas 4, 28, 33, 140
papaya 35, 46, 86, 120
parsnips 120
pasta 69, 89, 96, 121
pea 62, 121
pear 40, 46, 48–9, 51, 60, 121
    baked 89
pectin 48, 104, 106
pepper 69, 121
pepsin 20, 27
peristalsis 6, 34, 110
pesto 70, 78
pickles 28
pineapple 121–2
porridge 35, 46, 49, 98
potassium 65, 106
potatoes 23, 26, 33, 100, 122
probiotics 138
protein 3, 4–6, 12, 25, 27–8, 33, 42
prunes 37, 47, 122, 139
puddings 31, 89–94
pulses 122–3
pumpkin 123

quinoa 123

raisins 123
raspberry 123
raw foods 39, 44, 139
redcurrants 123
refined foods 7, 23, 32, 33
regularity 20
relaxing 31–2, 34, 95
rhubarb 124
rice 12, 40, 70, 124
    recipes 40, 56, 61, 88
rocket 33, 78, 89
rosewater 47, 67
royal jelly 142
rye 124

saffron 70, 82
saliva 4, 7, 8, 23, 40

salmon recipes 51, 84, 85
salsa verde 77
salt 65, 125
sauces 48, 76–80
sauerkraut 28
seaweed 69, 70
self-denial 22
sesame 80, 125
sex 33
slippery elm 40, 41, 47, 140
snacks 100
soups 62, 72–6
soya 125
spinach 33, 53, 60
    and fennel soup 72
starch 26–7, 33, 38, 64, 96
stock 36, 41, 46, 49–51, 70
stomach ulcers 68, 103
store cupboard 65–71
strawberry 125–6
stress 12, 13, 20, 26, 29, 31–2, 42–3, 97,
    139, 142
sugar 7, 22, 96, 126
sunflower 126
super-foods 36, 46, 141–2
supplements 10, 13, 25, 28, 46, 137–42
sweet potato 126–7
sweeteners 71, 100–1

tahini 71
tea 127
tekka 71
tiredness 13, 27, 29, 32, 44, 46
tobacco 22, 139, 143
tomato 35, 127

tomato ketchup 101
toxicity 2, 3–5, 6, 8, 25, 143
Transitibiane 47, 140
trout, smoked 60

Udo's Digestive Enzyme 35, 36, 47, 139
Udo's Oil 36, 46, 47, 67, 69, 99
Udo's Super-5 35, 36, 47, 138

vegetarian diet 10–11
vegetable stock 50, 70
vegetables 10, 12, 25, 27, 44, 46, 71, 95,
    96, 111, 124
    for constipation 33
    cooking 29
    for diarrhoea 39
    stir-fry 63, 66
vinegar 65
Vitam-R 71
vitamins 2, 6, 10, 141
volume of food 5, 29, 40, 45, 96

walnut 127
water 19, 34, 35, 40, 46, 67, 69, 100,
    128–9
watercress 33, 129
wheat 15, 26, 69, 96, 129–30
whey 28, 142, 144
wind 15–16, 17, 18–19, 25, 33, 41, 46, 75,
    96, 140
wine 103
work-outs, mind/body 32

yoghurt 35, 41, 95, 98, 131
    recipes 79, 91